THE
Secret
OF THE
Butterfly
Lovers

THE
Secret
OF THE
Butterfly
Lovers

Eternal Lessons of Life, Love, and Reincarnation

Keith Richardson

WEISER BOOKS
San Francisco, CA / Newburyport, MA

First published in 2007 by
Red Wheel/Weiser, LLC

With offices at:
500 Third Street, Suite 230
San Francisco, CA 94107
www.redwheelweiser.com

ISBN-10: 1-57863-395-8
ISBN-13: 978-1-57863-395-1

LIBRARY OF CONGRESS CATALOGING-IN-PUBLICATION DATA
AVAILABLE UPON REQUEST

Cover and text design by Maxine Ressler
Typeset in Fournier MT
Cover photograph © Romy Ragan

Printed in Canada
TCP
10 9 8 7 6 5 4 3 2 1

CONTENTS

ACKNOWLEDGMENTS

The Secret of the Butterfly Lovers took me five years to put together
and write. Unlike fiction, where you can control the pace of the writing, with nonfiction you can't rush. You have to wait for the story to
happen and then write it down. Much of my time spent on this book
consisted of receiving messages from my spirit guide Chang and then
researching these messages using historical reference books or just
waiting for Chang's predictions to come true.

I wish to first thank Francesca, my wife of thirty-two years, for her
patience and understanding for the many hours I abandoned her to
write four books over the past decade. Without the "true love" she
has for me I could never have completed even one of these books.

I next give thanks to the members of my soul group, "The Circle
of One." This group not only supported me while I put this book
together, but they also helped me by reading and rereading drafts
of this book and giving me valuable advice regarding typos, chapter
placement, and the accuracy of its stories. I particularly wish to thank
Kathy Rosengren and Brenda Ball for their participation on my quest
to write this book.

Along with my friends in my soul group, I also acknowledge my
soul group enemies. These people have taught me many valuable lessons in this life and in past lives. I send these people love and forgive-
ness for all the wrongs they have done to me.

My sons Keith William and Kevin also get my special thanks. Keith
is a professional computer programmer. He helped me set up a web
site for *The Secret of the Butterfly Lovers*. Kevin used his expertise
as a newspaper editor to help me with the details and key points of
my book. His honest critique of my writing style and his suggestions

about every chapter were a key factor in getting my book accepted for publication.

Finally I wish to thank my spirit guide Chang. Meeting him five years ago has changed my life. Chang has supported the writing of this book from its inception. He has also prodded me to continue to work on the book when I have become diverted with other projects or just lost interest. Like the ghost of the sea captain in the book *The Ghost and Mrs. Muir,* Chang has shown me the images of success and abundance. With this ongoing help in writing this book, his predictions are now becoming a reality.

The other day while taking a walk in my neighborhood, my wife Francesca spotted a hummingbird following us. For Francesca a hummingbird is a sign sent from heaven from my mother Marguerite who passed away in September of 1997. My mother never saw any of my books in print, but she was my biggest advocate for becoming an author. I asked Chang about the significance of this omen and he told me the hummingbird was a sign from my mother that *The Secret of the Butterfly Lovers* was going to be a very significant book that would ultimately change the world.

Life Is a Quest

As I have walked through my journey of life, I have come to realize that there is a plan and purpose for everything. It is each one of us who makes this plan and it is each one of us who fulfills this purpose. When our plans and purposes are not fulfilled, we need only look to ourselves for blame.

Our souls have many choices as to how they exist in the universe. We may exist as stardust in infinite clouds in the voids of space for billions of years. We may also choose to be a massive redwood tree and grow tall and wide for thousands of years. The existence you and I chose, however, was a small human form that rarely lives longer than one hundred revolutions of the earth around the sun.

As humans, we have a very short time to discover and fulfill our missions. Many of us get so lost in our mundane lives with our prideful endeavors that we never even figure out what we are here for. And we never begin a personal quest to accomplish this mission.

For a number of years I, like most people, was caught up in the cycle of self-fulfillment and making ends meet on a day-to-day basis. I didn't care about the spiritual realm because I did not think it had anything to do with my life or the world I lived in. I viewed everything as a logical formula of A+B=C; if I work hard and I save my money, I can live a good life in this world.

Then, in 1994, my life and my perception of reality underwent a tremendous change. I lost my job and left a profession I had excelled at for twenty years. By default I became the proprietor of a spiritual gift store and art gallery in Ventura, California, called Things From Heaven. In this position I learned many new things about life and began to question the underlying philosophy behind my traditional work ethic.

Since that time I have written and published three spiritual books and traveled throughout the world to speak on the topic of spirituality. In the process I have also learned new lessons about life and myself. The most important lesson I learned is about love. I know now that fear and hate are only an illusion and that love is the only truth in the universe. Whether you are stardust, a tree, or a human being, love is the only reality you need.

This book you hold in your hands will take you on a journey of life and love. It is a story about my journey, but it is also your journey. It is the journey of all souls in the universe. It is a journey of finding love and happiness. It is about my quest, but it is also about your quest to find your own path to heaven.

To discover your path you must open your eyes to a new spiritual realm. This process is an adventure that will allow your heart to accept the gift of "true love" that God wants you to have.

The Butterfly Lovers—
A Chinese Legend

OVER 1,700 YEARS AGO, near the end of the Jin Dynasty, in what is today the Zhejiang Province of China, two young people met and fell in love while attending school. The tale of their undying love has today become a cherished legend throughout the country of China.

Zhu Ying Tai was a beautiful sixteen-year-old girl with long flowing black hair and sparkling brown eyes. She was studious and eager to learn. She broke the mold of traditional women in her society by choosing a formal education over learning basic household chores.

Liangshan Bo was a tall, handsome eighteen-year-old man. He was the top student in his class and had big dreams for his future. He came from a poor family who had struggled to pay for his education. They felt that his hard work and accomplishments in school would allow him to find a better vocation in life and thus increase their family's wealth and social status.

Ying Tai felt mysteriously drawn to the intelligent and charming Bo as soon as she met him. She soon fell madly in love with him. When she told Bo how she felt about him, he admitted that he had the same feelings toward her. They believed that their love was predestined and would last forever.

At first, Ying Tai kept her love of Bo a secret from her family, but after nearly a year, she decided to tell him to ask her parents for her hand in marriage. Ying Tai felt certain that her parents would understand the meaning of "true love."

When Ying Tai told her mother and father about her feelings for Bo, they were furious. Unbeknown to Ying Tai, her family and Bo's were engaged in a long-standing feud. Furthermore, the Ling family was of a much higher social and economic status than Bo's. It would be a disgrace to her parents for her to marry someone from a family as despised and as poor as his.

On learning of Ying Tai's intent to marry Bo, her parents quickly arranged for her to wed a man from a wealthy family who they felt would form a better alliance and thus would bring them increased social status and prosperity.

Ying Tai was heartbroken when she learned what her parents had done. Not only did she not love the man chosen for her, she had also never met him. She knew deep in her soul that she could only be happy with Bo, her true love.

When Bo came to Ying Tai's parents to ask for her hand in marriage, her father told him a cruel lie. He said that Ying Tai had suffered a serious illness and had died the night before. Bo was devastated. He knew he could never be happy without his true love by his side. In a fit of grief, he drank a cup of poison and died. After his death, Bo was buried in a tomb near Ying Tai's home.

When Ying Tai learned of the lie her parents had told Bo and its horrible consequences, she was grief stricken. She knew, however, that she had to follow her parents' wishes in order to maintain the honor of her family. She picked out a beautiful wedding dress that made her look like a golden butterfly.

Her parents arranged an elaborate wedding celebration that fit their new social status. They also purchased an elegant sedan, gilded in gold, and commissioned their four strongest servants to carry Ying Tai to her wedding ceremony.

Ying Tai made just one request of her parents, as a condition for accepting the arranged marriage. She asked that the wedding procession pass by the cemetery where her true love, Liangshan Bo, was buried.

The day of the marriage finally arrived and Ying Tai's parents were thrilled by the excellent alliance they had made. As the wedding procession passed the gates of the cemetery, Ying Tai jumped out of her wedding sedan and ran to the tomb. There, she fell to her knees and cried.

As she knelt there crying, the wind began to blow and clouds filled the sky. Then suddenly a bright flash of light and a clap of thunder filled the air. A lightning bolt came down from the heavens and hit Bo's tomb. The explosion caused the ground to shake and cracked open the tomb, creating a passageway into the grave.

In an act of total despair, Ying Tai jumped through the crack to her death, deep inside the tomb. The once jubilant wedding party was now shocked and filled with grief. Zhu Ying Tai's greedy parents suddenly felt shame for the terrible thing they had done to Liangshan Bo, and for the ordeal they had forced their daughter to suffer through.

What happened next amazed and inspired everyone. Out of the death pit, where the two tragic lovers now lay, flew two beautiful golden butterflies. The butterflies danced happily in the air. They then flew up into the clouds together and vanished into heaven.

To this day, the people of China believe that the two butterflies were the undaunted spirits of the lovers who had at last found true love, and were now free from the greed and prejudice of their world below.

The tale of the "Butterfly Lovers" is one of the most popular legends in China. It has been called the Chinese "Romeo and Juliet." Over the centuries, this story has been adapted into traditional operas, movies, television programs, and even a concerto.

For many years there has been great debate over the origin of the story and the city in which it took place, which has affected the story's application for a World Heritage listing. A recent archeological dig excavated a

1,700-year-old tomb, which is believed to belong to Liangshan Bo. This evidence helped to prove where the story took place and that the "Butterfly Lovers" legend is truly a cultural legacy for the Chinese people.

All regions with records and relics related to this story worked together to prepare a report for the Chinese Ministry of Culture. In 2006, this report was transferred to UNESCO, which sanctioned this tale as an official cultural legacy of China.

When I first heard this tale from a Chinese tourist visiting my store, I was intrigued by its simple poignancy. I had no idea at the time what this would come to mean to my wife and myself and of the life-changing adventure it would lead us on.

Because my story is necessarily intertwined with the life story of others, out of respect for people's privacy I have changed a few names.

THE
Secret
OF THE
Butterfly
Lovers

CHAPTER ONE

Meeting Chang

I AM A TRAINED SCIENTIST WITH a master's degree in cultural anthropology. I have conducted field research in Latin America and Asia. I have published articles in professional journals and spoken at national anthropological conferences.

For over a decade, my wife Francesca and I have owned and operated an angel-themed gift shop in Ventura, California, called Things From Heaven. Working in this store, I have documented many amazing spiritual events. These include visions of angels, spontaneous healings, and conversations with lost loved ones on the other side. I have published three books documenting these phenomena.

The most amazing and life-changing experiences I have had, however, occurred due to what appeared to be an accidental contact with a spiritual guide named Chang. This book documents the revelations I have received from this highly evolved spiritual entity.

❀ A Guided Meditation by John Edward

In January of 2001, I purchased what I thought was a book on tape, called *Understanding Your Angels and Meeting Your Guides* by psychic John Edward. John Edward was very popular at the time with national daytime and evening talk shows. His concept of communicating with people's deceased loved ones using participants from a television studio audience was a new and exciting concept that had everyone talking about heaven again. I thought it would be good to learn more about Mr. Edward's opinions about angels so I could better discuss them with people who visited my store.

Francesca and I always go to a gift show at the Los Angeles Convention Center in mid-January, and I thought it would be interesting to listen to this tape while we drove to the gift show. I waited until we got on the freeway to put the tape in our car's player, and then I heard something that really disappointed me. The voice on the tape said, "Please don't listen to this tape while driving your car. This is a guided meditation."

At first I was furious. I had purchased this tape with the single intent of listening to it on our way to Los Angeles.

I felt I had wasted my money and considered returning the tape for a refund. I angrily ejected the tape from the player and threw it on the floor in the back of my car. It sat there for the next month.

On a Tuesday in mid-February of 2001, Francesca and I had the day off with nothing important to do. I suggested that we try to listen to the guided meditation by John Edward. I found it still lying on the floor of my car where I had thrown it. We turned off all the lights, unplugged the telephone, and sat on our couch. I figured I would get my money's worth out of this tape yet.

The tape started out with a discussion of chakras. I was immediately frustrated, as I was only really interested in what John Edward had to say about angels. And then he said something that concerned me even more. Communicating with your angels was not that important, he declared, which was why his meditation was about "spirit guides" instead.

"Spirit guides? I don't even believe in spirit guides. This tape really is stupid. I have wasted my money and now I'm wasting my time," I thought to myself.

Despite my concerns, I grudgingly decided to do the meditation anyway. John Edward first led me to meet my "spirit animal." To my surprise, an animal did come to meet me. It was my dog Shauna, who had died three years before. At first I was really happy to see my little dog in such good shape as she ran to meet me. Then I thought to myself, "This is stupid. Of course I'm going to see my dog. It's all just wishful thinking. There's nothing real about this vision at all."

John Edward's voice led me to follow my dog down a beautiful wooded path, past a bubbling spring, and finally into a clearing covered with bright green grass. In the middle of this clearing was a small wooden cabin. I followed my dog to the door of the cabin. At this point she left me and went frolicking through the grass and disappeared back into the forest.

John Edward directed me to knock on the door of the cabin. He said that I would meet my spirit guide when the door opened.

"Why am I doing this?" I asked myself. "I don't believe in this sort of thing. It's the stuff that crazy people tell you about. Yeah, everyone has this really cool Native American spirit guide that gives them messages. People should learn to accept responsibility for their own actions. They should learn to think for themselves and not have to rely on silly invisible friends like spirit guides."

But I had gone too far now to turn back, so I knocked at the door of the cabin and shortly thereafter it began to slowly open. As I looked at the person standing in the doorway, I was stunned. It was not who I had expected at all. It was a tall, thin-faced Asian man who appeared to be in his late fifties or early sixties, and looked a little like the mythical character Fu Manchu.

He had a long, thin mustache that hung down each side of his mouth, he had a goatee on his chin, and his head was bald with the exception of a long ponytail. He wore a strange double-decker hat that had a blue brim with a yellow band around it. The upper portion was red, topped by a large gold pointed spike. He wore a yellow robe with dragons embroidered on it. He clasped his hands together and politely bowed to me.

I was shocked. "I must be eating too much Chinese food. Everyone has a really cool spirit guide. And for some reason I'm stuck with one that looks like Fu Manchu."

Then John Edward said that I should ask my guide his name. "What's your name?" I asked sarcastically.

"Chang," the tall Asian man standing in front of me replied.

"I really have been eating too much Chinese food," I thought. "I've met Chang King."

John Edward suggested that I ask my guide what my life mission was. I halfheartedly complied.

Chang opened his robe and pulled out a copy of a book that I had written in 1997 called *Andy Lakey's Psychomanteum*. I was surprised at first, but then I concluded, "Of course I'm going to see my book. I must be on some sort of ego trip or something."

John Edward talks pretty fast, and the tape wound down before I had a chance to ask Chang any more questions. I asked Francesca what she saw, and she responded, "I can't meditate. I didn't see anything at all."

Then I made what I would at first feel was a big mistake. I told Francesca of my encounter with Chang. She was intrigued and extremely excited by my vision. This soon became an embarrassment for me, as she would tell all of our friends and her relatives, "It's so exciting! Keith has a spirit guide. We think he's Chinese; his name is Chang."

I eventually confronted my wife: "Francesca, why do you keep telling people about this? Aren't you afraid that they're going to think I'm crazy? People are going to start thinking that I am getting stressed out from working too hard and suggest that I receive psychiatric help."

"Keith, your spirit guide is very important to you. You are receiving this message for a reason. Everyone has to know about him," she answered.

I insisted that it all seemed pretty meaningless to me, and I had probably just imagined him anyway.

"Look Keith," said Francesca, "I've had many spiritual experiences since we've known each other. You've always thought I was imagining these things or that I was crazy. Now that you're having these kinds of experiences too, you'll have to believe the things I tell you. I know you didn't imagine him. I know that Chang is real."

❁ Ghost Hunters

In March of 2001, a friend of ours named Richard Senate came into our store. Richard is a local "ghost buster" who has written many books about hauntings in Ventura. He also has appeared on many television programs, including *The Merv Griffin Show*, *Sightings*, and *Haunted History*.

"I've got some great news," said Richard. "I have just been hired by Adelphia Cable to host a nationally syndicated program called *Ghost Hunters*. I would like both of you to help me put together a show about angels."

Francesca and I were excited and quite honored by the invitation. We quickly agreed to do the program. Richard made just one request of us: that we bring someone on the show who had had a real angel experience at our store.

❁ Katherine's Spirit Guide

Francesca and I debated possible candidates for the program over the next few days. I felt that the only person fit to represent us on television was a woman named Katherine Rosengren. Katherine had credibility.

Katherine is a small woman with short blond hair, twinkling blue eyes, and a sweet smile that radiates positive energy wherever she goes. Besides having an excellent presence, Katherine has the credentials to back her up. She is a registered nurse, with three master's degrees in psychology. She was also the Director of Volunteer Services at a local hospice for ten years. Besides this, she is married to a medical doctor in Ventura and assists him in his practice.

On two different occasions, with five different people, Katherine experienced angelic presences at our store. Her amazing stories are described in two of my books.

I called Katherine, and she agreed to do the program. We filmed our show at Adelphia Studios in Oxnard, California, on an evening in early April of 2001. Katherine did an incredible job of describing her angel experiences. She was a natural on camera, speaking with sincerity and professional conviction. Her participation helped us to make this one of the best programs of the *Ghost Hunters* series. It continued to be aired on Adelphia Cable stations throughout the United States as I wrote this book.

After the filming, Francesca and I invited Katherine out to dinner. We went to a casual restaurant that had a sports bar in it. There was a basketball game playing on their big screen television and the fans were howling like a pack of hungry wolves. I felt that this would be a perfect atmosphere where we could talk about anything we wanted and no one would hear us.

"Katherine, you were fantastic tonight," I told her. "I can't believe how many people have angelic experiences whenever you're around them."

Katherine looked at me over the table and smiled. "I never had many spiritual experiences in my life until the day I met my spirit guide."

Francesca looked at Katherine, very excited, and said, "You know what? Keith has a spirit guide, too!"

I knocked my knee against Francesca's under the table, looked at her sternly, clenched my teeth, and quickly shook my head. I did not want our friend to think I was crazy. Katherine could admit to a spirit guide if she wished, but I really did not want to give out this kind of information about myself to anyone.

Trying to keep my composure, I looked back at Katherine and said, "So what kind of spirit guide do you have? Is he a Native American, an African shaman, or maybe Merlin the magician?"

Unmoved by my ridicule, Katherine said, "My spirit guide is very unusual. I think he's Chinese."

This revelation caught me off guard. I felt as if someone had hit me on the head with a brick. I took a deep breath and timidly asked what he looked like.

"He kind of looks like . . . Fu Manchu." She stopped and looked at me, a little embarrassed, and then began again: "Well, um, he has a thin mustache that goes down his face, and a goatee on his chin. He wears a funny hat that looks like it is two stories or something, with a spike on top of it. He also wears a long, robe. It's funny . . . whenever I see him he always bows to me."

I felt a chill go down my spine. This was way too weird. How could Katherine see the same exact person that I had seen in the guided meditation with John Edward two months earlier?

"What is your spirit guide's name?" I stammered.

Katherine looked a little perplexed. She thought for a moment and said, "Well, I couldn't communicate with my guide at first. He would appear to me whenever I did a healing massage on one of my hospice patients. I was finally so intrigued by his appearance that I booked a session with a psychic named Michael. I asked him about what I was seeing. Michael told me that my spirit guide's name was . . . Ch-Ch-Chang."

I leaned back in my chair in shock, unable to speak for a moment. I felt as if the room was spinning around me. I had not taken my experience seriously, yet here was someone I did not know that well, and she had seen the same manifestation, with the same name as the man I had seen in my meditation.

I shook my head. I could feel my heart pounding loudly as I tried to speak. I cleared my throat and said, "This is really, really strange. My spirit guide's name is also Chang and he looks exactly like the Chinese person you just described."

Katherine gasped and sat back stiff in her chair, stunned by my revelation.

I tried to compose myself, and asked Katherine one more question: "Did Michael tell you what your mission was?"

"Yes he did," said Katherine, now seemingly more confident. "There are supposed to be seventeen people throughout the world who have Chang as their spirit guide. Some of us will become famous and others of us will remain unknown. All of us will have the same mission to accomplish: 'Helping the people of the world to overcome their fear of death and helping bring peace and love to the world.' As a spiritual counselor and a hospice worker, I practice these things daily."

"Oh, my God," I responded, "That's what Chang was trying to tell me. My mission is to write spiritual books. The theme of all my books is to show people how to overcome their fear of death and to find greater love for one another. Katherine, how many of these seventeen people do you know?"

"Just you," she replied, "I think we may be destined to do something together. Don't you?"

"What do you think it is we have to do?" I asked.

She smiled and said, "I don't know yet, but I'm sure we'll learn our tasks in due time."

The three of us completed our dinner together, and Francesca and I dropped Katherine off at her home in Ventura. As we drove home, Francesca and I were so dumbfounded by the evening's events that we did not know what to say to one another. We just kept repeating, "That was really weird, really, really weird."

When we arrived home, Francesca asked me, "Keith, what do you think this all means?"

I shrugged. "I don't know. Maybe it was just a really strange coincidence."

Francesca shook her head vigorously and said, "What's wrong with you Keith? Can't you see there's too much happening for this to be a coincidence? You both saw the same spirit guide and received the same exact message. Something like this could never ever happen by coincidence."

I nodded grudgingly. "You're probably right. There's just too much going on here to write this off. I wonder what, if anything, this will lead to."

Francesca smiled at me and said very seriously, "Keith, don't you know this is all going to lead to our destiny?"

I laughed at her solemn tone, "So what do you think our destiny is?"

"I don't know, but I think we are going to find out soon," she replied.

✺ James Van Praagh Knows Chang

In the summer of 2002, strange things began to happen again. Francesca and I went to a wholesale book outlet and made a major purchase of spiritual books to sell in our store. One of the books that we purchased was a bestselling autobiography entitled *Talking to Heaven* by psychic James Van Praagh. I was never particularly impressed by Van Praagh, so the book held little interest for me at first.

For some reason, however, Francesca became fascinated to the point of obsession by this book. She just couldn't put it down. She carried it with her everywhere, and to my annoyance, quoted passages to me wherever we went. I was on my computer attempting to answer an e-mail from a customer about my Website, when Francesca came into the room holding Van Praagh's book and crying. Tears ran down her cheeks and she looked like she had seen a ghost.

"Stop what you're doing," she demanded.

"What's the matter?" I asked, concerned.

"I've just found something very important. I think it's going to change our lives," she sobbed. "It's Chang! He's James Van Praagh's spirit guide too."

She handed me her copy of *Talking to Heaven* and said, "Read this, Keith."

"Can't you see I'm really busy? I'll read it later," I protested.

"No!" she responded firmly, "This is really important. You can't put this off. You've got to read it right now."

"Well, okay, give it to me," I gave in.

Francesca opened the book to chapter three, "Spiritual Helpers," and turned the page to the sub-chapter "Becoming Aware of My Guides."

My hands began to tremble as I read the words on the page. I really couldn't believe what I was seeing. I thought Chang was more of a personal experience for me and maybe Katherine too, with a few coincidences thrown in, but this showed me that there was something real about the vision I had the year before.

Van Praagh recounted that while he was in a psychic session with a British clairvoyant named Irene Martin-Giles, he had been told that a Chinese man named Chang was his spiritual teacher. The clairvoyant added that Chang had come through many times to deliver messages to Van Praagh for his clients.

As they went further into their psychic session, the clairvoyant began to draw a picture of Chang, which Van Praagh went on to describe. He said that Chang wore a small cap with an orange top and a blue brim. He was draped in a robe and his hands were interlocked in its sleeves. Chang's face was long and narrow and his eyes were brown and gave a sense of gentleness. He wore a traditional ponytail, and a majestic goatee alleviated the stark baldness of his head. Van Praagh then went on to say that Chang was of the highest spiritual realm, and that he was a true master guide.

❀ Nancy's Reading

I went on the internet and looked up James Van Praagh, to see if I could find anything else about Chang. There was nothing there of significance, but I did find that Van Praagh had a new television program coming out in the fall called *Beyond*. I ordered tickets for Francesca, myself, and some of our friends to attend the taping of one of his first programs.

On Tuesday, September 9, 2002, we were set to go to the KTLA Studios in Hollywood, California, which is about an hour's drive from our home, to see *Beyond*. One person Francesca had felt had to go to see the show was our youngest son's girlfriend's mother, Nancy. But when our entire group met at our house to caravan to the studio together, Nancy was nowhere to be found.

Francesca, concerned, called Nancy, who said that she had decided not to go.

"I feel too depressed," she explained.

Francesca pleaded with her, until Nancy reluctantly agreed. About ten minutes later she arrived, dressed in white pants with a gold blazer. Her blond hair was tied back in a bun.

"You look really nice, Nancy," exclaimed Francesca. "I really don't know why you didn't want to go with us."

"I didn't feel up to going, but I'm glad I made it now," Nancy replied.

Our caravan of three vehicles set off to Hollywood to see Van Praagh's show. We arrived two hours early and parked in the KTLA lot. We walked to the studio and were instructed by the gate staff to wait in line outside the gate, next to a large shrub.

After we had waited over an hour and a half in the sun, the studio staff came to the gate and let our group, and the over one hundred other people in line, enter the main gate and stand in a covered holding area. From here we were ushered into the television studio.

The studio featured a large stadium-style seating area. From the back, it looked rickety. It was made of a bare wood frame, reminiscent of a poorly built porch deck. From the front, however, it looked like a beautiful auditorium, with a big screen television perched above a colorfully painted walkway through which the host of the show could enter.

Getting to the seating area was somewhat difficult and treacherous. We worked our way carefully to our seats in the right corner of the seating area. Nancy sat to my left, Francesca to my right.

Shortly after we were seated, James Van Praagh entered the set. Van Praagh, a rather short man, middle-aged with a mustache, addressed the audience kindly and sincerely. He thanked us all for coming to see his new show and then asked us to participate in a guided meditation.

Growing up in the Los Angeles area, I had attended the filming of many television programs, but I had never been asked to participate in a meditation before. I felt that this added touch showed the honesty and integrity of the host. Due to this, and other things that happened on this program, I gained a new respect for James Van Praagh that day.

Shortly after the meditation, the filming of *Beyond* began. There was musical fanfare and an introduction by Van Praagh to the program's mission: Helping people understand that their loved ones on the other side were all right and that death was nothing to fear.

Van Praagh then stopped suddenly, looked at the audience, and said, "There's someone here today who didn't want to come, but a friend dragged her here."

Upon hearing this, our friend Nancy slumped down into her chair, clasped her arms together and looked tensely at Van Praagh. Francesca nudged her and whispered, "I think he's talking about you." Nancy just tightened her jaw and shook her head.

Undaunted, Van Praagh looked at the audience once more and said "I know there's someone here today in the audience who did not want to come, but a friend dragged her here." He then pointed at Nancy and said, "I feel the energy coming from you. Were you dragged here today by a friend?"

Nancy shyly nodded her head. "Francesca dragged me here," she said, pointing at my wife. "I really didn't want to come."

Van Praagh paused for a moment, and looked directly at Nancy as he said, "What's your connection with Phoenix?"

Gaining her composure, Nancy answered, "I don't have any connection with Phoenix at all."

"Didn't you just purchase a plane ticket?" inquired Van Praagh.

"Yes, I did, I'm going to Albuquerque," Nancy stated defiantly.

"Tell me, where does your flight connect?" Van Praagh persisted.

"Oh my God, you're right. My plane stops in Phoenix and then connects to Albuquerque," Nancy responded with astonishment.

Van Praagh continued, "You're going to visit someone who has cancer, aren't you?"

"Yes, my cousin," Nancy answered.

Van Praagh looked at her with compassion in his eyes and said, "I'm sorry to tell you this, but your cousin isn't going to make it."

Nancy was too numb by this point to react to the bad news. She just said, "This is why I didn't want to come here today. I didn't want to find this out."

Van Praagh had stopped speaking. He appeared to be listening to something. He looked at Nancy intensely and asked, "Who's Margaret?"

Nancy looked shocked. "She's my best friend. How do you know about her?"

"Has her father passed?" asked Van Praagh.

"Yes, he died two months ago."

"Margaret's father says that he wants her to get along with her brother," he said.

"Oh, my God, Margaret hates her brother," blurted Nancy.

Then Van Praagh received a message from Nancy's mother. He relayed her description of Nancy's bedroom, saying that it had a window that overlooked their garden, wood paneling, and spiritual paintings on the walls.

The hot water had gone off in my home the month before going to the show, and Francesca and I had used Nancy's upstairs bathroom shower. So, I knew what their bedroom looked like. I also knew that the spiritual paintings described on the walls were the Andy Lakey angel paintings we had given Nancy and her husband, Ted, for Christmas the year before.

I was now in shock as well. "Wow, this guy's really good," I thought to myself. "This has to be real."

Nancy visited her cousin in Albuquerque the next week. She said that she had always been afraid of flying, but the messages from James Van Praagh helped her to have one of the most pleasant flights ever. Her cousin died of cancer two months later, as Van Praagh had predicted.

Our encounter with James Van Praagh was very inspirational, and helped to validate our belief in life after death. But it did not answer many of our questions about Chang. It would still be a few years before we would be able to find what this connection with Van Praagh was all about.

CHAPTER TWO

Almost Famous in Japan

I HAVE BEEN INSPIRED TO WRITE books ever since we opened our store in 1995. Before that, I had written articles for newspapers and for professional newsletters for hospitals that I did fundraising for, but I had never been inspired enough to take on an entire book. I now feel that it was my spirit guide Chang that brought me to open my store and it was also Chang that led me to write all of my books.

I self-published my first book, *Andy Lakey's Psychomanteum*, in September of 1997. The book describes how we founded our store, Things From Heaven, and how we got Andy Lakey's art in our store. It also tells about the miracles that happened with this art. These miracles included healings—of everything from AIDS to cancer—and the receipt of messages from deceased loved ones.

I paid for everything myself for this book. This included professional editing, cover design, printing of five thousand copies, shipping and distribution costs, and hiring a public relations firm to promote it.

Despite all of my efforts, my book never did really take off the way I wanted it to. I had a whole garage full of my self-published books and very minimal book sales. To make things even worse, the distributing company I had contracted with went bankrupt and I lost over one thousand of my books in the process. It seemed unlikely that I would ever be picked up by a major publishing company, let alone make any money selling my books. My spirit guide, however, had other ideas about my life's mission, and other plans for my book's future.

❀ Hanna's Mission

By early November of 2000, three years after my book had come out, I had just about lost interest in the idea of ever writing a book again. Then one day, a regular customer named Sherry brought her sister-in-law Hanna, a Japanese woman, to visit our store.

Sherry was an American woman in her late forties. She had light brown hair and a warm smile. Hanna was a tall and thin Japanese woman with short black hair. She appeared to be in her early forties, and seemed tense and very serious.

Sherry was excited to show Hanna around, and asked me to personally give her the grand tour. I was honored to show Hanna around, but was soon concerned by her responses. Every time I showed her something, she would reply, "I'm sorry, but I really don't like angels that much."

I finally took Hanna to the art gallery in the back of our store and showed her the angel art by Andy Lakey. She took a moment to look at the artworks and finally said, "It's pretty, but it's really not my style."

I found Hanna to be fairly blunt and to the point, but I really was not offended by her reactions. "You can't please everyone," I thought to myself as she and her sister-in-law finally left our store, and I went on with my business.

About a week later, I began getting very unusual e-mails from a person who said she had read my book, *Andy Lakey's Psychomanteum*. The first message read, "What did you mean when you said, on page thirty-two of your book, that the phenomenon people experience at your store with the art of Andy Lakey is not a local occurrence?"

At first this question intimidated me. "Was this some sort of religious fanatic trying to debunk my book?" I wondered. I almost deleted the e-mail, but then I thought, "If someone has taken the time to read my book, I owe them the courtesy of responding to their questions and concerns."

I gave my answer to this question much time and thought, and then sent it to the inquisitive person. "Well, that takes care of that," I said to myself. The next day, however, there was a question about a different topic on another page of my book. "This person isn't giving up. I'll show her, I'll answer all of her questions until she runs out of questions, or just plain loses interest," I grudgingly thought.

This intellectual exercise went on for over a month. I began to look forward to answering the next challenging question that this person had for me. In mid-December of 2000, I received a phone call that would explain what all the questions were about. The voice on the other end of the line said, "Hello, this is Hanna. Maybe you don't remember me, but I am the Japanese woman who came to your store last month with my sister-in-law Sherry. I'm also the one who has been e-mailing you about your book."

"Why have you been contacting me so much?" I asked.

"I read your book, it's changed my life, and I feel that it has to be translated into Japanese," she answered.

"How did you come to read my book?" I asked.

"Well," Hanna began, "I had come to spend a week with my sister-in-law Sherry from my home in Washington State. She told me that your store was one of her favorite places, and took me to see it. I was not that impressed at first, because I'm not very religious and I really don't believe in angels. When we returned to Sherry's home, we talked about spirituality and angels for a while. My sister-in-law then gave me a copy of your book. I took it just to be polite. I really didn't intend to read it."

I was not sure where she was going with this, but I let her continue.

"When I arrived at Los Angeles International Airport to catch my flight back to Seattle, I found that my flight had a two-hour delay. So I began to read your book. I became intrigued by your stories. I just couldn't put it down. I knew this was something I had to share with the people of Japan."

"I would be honored to have you translate my book into Japanese," I said. "But what are your qualifications to do this?"

"Before I married Sherry's brother and came to the United States, I was involved in the television industry in Tokyo. I did translations and voiceovers for television programs and commercials," Hanna said. "I still have contacts in the media in Tokyo and I feel that I can bring your book and the art of Andy Lakey there, and make both of you successful."

I was impressed by Hanna's answer and later signed an agreement to let her translate my book. We worked together on this project for about two months, and in the end Hanna had a draft of my book that she felt would be presentable to her media contacts in Japan.

In March of 2001, Hanna went to Japan with the draft of my book and several pieces of art by Andy Lakey. She set meetings and made presentations to several of her major media contacts. She found, to her disappointment, that most of her contacts were not interested in the topic of angels and spirituality. Those that did show an interest in the art tried to go around Hanna and deal directly with Andy Lakey. Hanna returned from Japan sad, and very disappointed.

"You have a very important book, with a very important message and I can't believe that no one in Japan is interested in it," she said.

"When the time comes for my book and Andy Lakey's art to be in Japan, it will get there," I said, consolingly. "There doesn't seem to be anything that you, or I, or anyone else can do about this." I truly felt that my book and Andy Lakey's art would never be accepted in Japan. But I was wrong.

❀ Lavanaha's Inspiration

About a week later, a woman who said her name was Lavanaha came into our store for the first time. She appeared to be in her mid-fifties, and was very thin and tall, with long sandy blond hair tied in a ponytail.

Lavanaha had never seen or heard of the art of Andy Lakey, but she was very intrigued when she saw it. I told her about my book.

"I don't read books," she said.

"Maybe you've seen Andy Lakey on TV. He's been on many television shows," I continued.

Lavanaha shook her head. "I don't watch television."

"This art has been featured in many newspapers and magazines. He's been in the *Los Angeles Times*, the *New York Times*, and the *Christian Science Monitor*, as well as *Life* and *People* magazines."

Lavanaha again shook her head and said, "I don't read newspapers or magazines."

I was beginning to wonder what planet she was from, when she told me something that nearly knocked me down. "I work for an alternative healing organization out of Tokyo, Japan, called Japan Medical Arts. My office is in Santa Monica, California, but I fly to Japan every other month to give lectures. I feel that this art is very spiritual and healing, and I need to bring it to the attention of my company's executives in Tokyo."

Lavanaha did not buy my book, but instead purchased a copy of the beautifully illustrated coffee table book, *Andy Lakey Art, Angels & Miracles* by Andy Lakey and Paul Robert Walker.

❀ A Japanese Connection

About a month later, I received a phone call from Tokyo. It was Mr. Ogura, the international liaison of Japan Medical Arts (JMA). He wanted to visit my store and see Andy Lakey's art in person. He said that he would be able to be in Ventura on Wednesday of the following week. I agreed to meet with him, but I was very suspicious.

This was really too much of a coincidence for me. In less than one month, two different people had offered to bring Andy Lakey's art to Japan. I checked JMA out with Hanna. I found to my dismay that there was no connection with her, or her contacts, whatsoever.

The next week, Mr. Ogura visited our store with his wife. He was thin, short in stature, and appeared to be in his mid-fifties. He wore dress suit pants with a navy blue blazer. His wife was a petite and very pretty Japanese woman in her late forties. She was also dressed in formal business attire. Both appeared to be impressed by Andy Lakey's art and the miracles and healings attributed to it.

Out of this meeting we were able to set another meeting with the president and three other top officials of JMA, along with Andy Lakey and myself. The purpose of our meeting was to discuss having an art show in Japan. We all met two weeks later at the most elegant hotel in Ventura.

The other three executives of JMA were about the same build and stature as Mr. Ogura. They also wore the same style navy blue blazers. The meeting began innocently enough, with Mr. Ogura presenting a plan for an art show to be held in Tokyo in July of 2001. The plan included JMA's art needs as well as the prices they wished to pay and sell the art for. Andy Lakey and these men haggled and negotiated terms that would be in the best interest of all involved.

In the midst of this very formal business discussion, the president of JMA, Mr. Hayashi, came over to me and whispered in slightly broken English, "I very embarrassed to ask question, but do you have anything written in Japanese about Andy Lakey."

The question caught me off guard for a second. But then the thought hit me. I did have a copy of Hanna's manuscript of my book in a drawer back at my store.

"Yes, I do have something in Japanese," I said, "I'll get you and the other executives copies of this after our meeting."

After the meeting, I rushed back to the store and dug out Hanna's Japanese manuscript of my book from the drawer I had thrown it in. I took it to a local Kinko's and made five bound copies for the executives of JMA. They took the manuscripts and read them on the trip back to Japan.

Impressed with the stories in my book, they invited me to attend the art show with Andy Lakey in July of 2001. We were given the royal treatment by JMA. Andy and I did newspaper and magazine interviews and were even included on a local television program in Japanese. I felt that this really proved the value of my book and was confident that they would help me to get it published in Japanese, but I was wrong again.

Mr. Ogura accompanied me back to Narita International Airport in Tokyo when our show was over. As I was about to leave for my terminal, I asked him when he thought JMA would help me to get my book published in Japanese.

Mr. Ogura looked at me sadly and said, "I am very sorry to tell you that the JMA executives and I had a meeting about your book yesterday. We decided that your book talks too much about your store in Ventura, California. We feel that someone reading your book will want to buy Andy Lakey's art from you and not from us. It would be bad business for JMA to support the publication of your book in Japan."

I felt it was really outrageous that JMA would think that my little store in California would pose a great competitive risk for the entire country of Japan, but there was nothing I could say to dissuade Mr. Ogura. The decision had already been made. It seemed that my book would never be published in Japan. But I was still wrong.

CHAPTER THREE

A Message of Abundance

THE YEAR 2002 HAD BEEN pretty bad financially for my family and our store. The war in Afghanistan brought on by the September 11, 2001, attacks had dispirited the nation. Angels had fallen out of favor with the public, and our store's revenues fell significantly. It was our worst holiday season ever.

We ultimately had to borrow money on our credit cards to pay the rent and sales tax revenues. We could not come up with the money to pay for the goods for the holiday season. By January of 2003, our creditors were threatening to sue us.

As the prospect of war with Iraq became apparent, things got even worse. Our store is located in Ventura County, where the largest employers are military bases. Monies were diverted from these bases to pay for the war efforts. Civilian base personnel and subcontractors were laid off.

My oldest son Keith William had also lost his job due to this. Furthermore, he and his wife Leah's baby, our first grandson Kyler, was stillborn around the same time. For these reasons, Keith and Leah decided to sell their home in Simi Valley, California, which is about thirty miles from Ventura, and move in with us—a decision that further increased our financial burdens.

To make matters even worse, the entire economy of Ventura County began to suffer due to decreased tourism and the financial cutbacks at the military bases. A significant number of retailers in downtown Ventura could no longer make ends meet and were forced to close their doors for good. We were on the brink of being the next casualty of this financial depression that was enveloping us like a dark, ominous cloud.

❀ Janet's Awakening

In the midst of this financial turmoil, our friend Janet, an advertising executive from a local television station, came to visit us at our store. Janet is a Japanese-American woman in her early forties. She has long black hair and bright brown eyes. This day Janet was very excited about an opportunity she had for our store and us.

"Keith, how would you like to advertise your store on James Van Praagh's television show *Beyond*?" she asked. "It's on at 7:00 PM every weeknight. I think it would be the perfect market for your store."

"I really can't afford the advertising right now," I told her. "We're in dire straits financially. I am really interested in James Van Praagh—I think we have some sort of spiritual connection—but I just can't afford to advertise on his program."

"I'm sorry to hear about your financial situation, Keith. Everyone is telling me the same thing. This is a bad time for all of us," she said. Then she looked at me with a skeptical glance. "By the way, what kind of 'spiritual connection' do you have with James Van Praagh? Do you know him or something?"

I felt a little cornered and was sorry I had told Janet as much as I had. We considered her a friend, but she wasn't really in our inner circle and I had never shared anything spiritual with her before. I just did not know how she would take it.

"Well, I met Van Praagh at a party a couple of years ago. We spoke for a couple of minutes and he was cordial enough, but we really didn't bond or anything. I doubt he'd even know me if he saw me again. Francesca and I also were audience members on his television program last fall, but that's not my connection either."

"So what is your connection then?" Janet asked impatiently.

I paused for a moment and then said shyly, "We both share the same spirit guide." I felt as if a great weight had been taken off of my shoulders as I said this.

Janet looked at me strangely. "What did you say?"

I took a deep breath and said, "We both have the same spiritual entity working with us from heaven."

"What you're telling me is really weird, Keith. I didn't think I'd ever hear something like this coming from you," she said. "Have you considered taking some time off and getting away from your store for a while? I know you're under a lot of pressure with your finances and all. I think you've got to let up a little bit. It seems to be getting to you." She appeared very concerned.

I felt embarrassed by Janet's response. My stomach sunk like a rock as she continued to look at me sympathetically. I felt that I had made a really bad impression. I knew that I would have to tell her the whole story about Chang, whether she was ready to hear it or not. With a mix of sympathy and skepticism, she agreed to hear me out. I proceeded to tell Janet about my first encounter with Chang. I told her exactly what Chang looked like and what I thought my mission was. I also told her how Katherine Rosengren and James Van Praagh had met the same guide, with the same name, and were given the same mission. Janet seemed a little less concerned about me by the time she left our store, but I still figured that she thought I belonged in a mental institution.

Two days had gone by, and then, much to my surprise, Janet came to see me at our store. "There's something I have to talk to you about," she said seriously.

"I already told you, I don't have the money to advertise on the James Van Praagh show," I said.

"I didn't come to talk to you about advertising," she said. "I've come to talk to you about Chang."

A chill ran down my back and my jaw dropped. "When I left your store the other day, I really thought you were crazy. I've come to apologize to you for feeling this way about you. I believe now that what you were telling me might be real."

"Why do you believe me now?" I said feeling puzzled.

"I had a personal experience with Chang," Janet said shyly.

"When I left your store, I really felt sorry for you. I thought you were losing it. Yesterday, I went to see my friend Debbie. During our conversation she told me that she had a spirit guide. She had never told me anything like that before, and since you had just told me about your spirit guide the day before, I was very intrigued."

"What is her guide's name?" I asked.

"Chang," she said casually.

You could have knocked me down with a feather.

"She said that he was Chinese and had a long mustache, goatee, and a ponytail. She described him exactly the way you did. This is the weirdest thing that's ever happened to me," Janet said.

Two days later, Janet brought Debbie to our store to meet me. Debbie was a tall woman in her mid-thirties with strawberry-blond hair. Her eyes were dark blue and seemed to look right through you when she spoke. I immediately felt an affinity with her.

"So you've seen Chang too," I laughed. "What mission did he tell you to accomplish?"

"Well, I really don't know what my mission is, but I know that I was led to be here with you today. I feel that there are no coincidences and that I have been brought here for a reason," she replied.

"Why?" I asked.

"I think I'm supposed to teach you something," she answered.

Skeptically, I asked her what she thought she was supposed to teach me. "Well, I'm a licensed hypnotherapist and I teach classes about contacting guardian angels. I think you could use someone like me to teach angel classes at your store," she said confidently.

I smiled at her and gave her offer some thought. I knew we had to do something to bring people to our store. We had nothing to lose now and we could also use the extra money that the classes would bring in. So, I asked her, "When can you start?"

"I would like to begin the classes in three weeks," she replied. "This should give us time to sign up people to attend, and for me to put my materials together."

We began the classes on Thursday night, March 13, 2003, which was also the day after the Iraqi war began. Ten people showed up, along with Debbie, Francesca, and myself, making thirteen of us in total. I could tell it wasn't an earthshaking success, but it was a start. Our angel class appeared to be our last chance.

Debbie began the class with an introduction of the Eastern concept of the "chakra." She told us that chakras were energy wheels that are positioned throughout your body. Each chakra has its own colors and its own function to make your body, mind, and spirit work correctly. She also went on to explain how we could control our chakras through positive visualization to bring health, wealth, and love to our lives.

I had heard all the chakra stuff before and was not really impressed. "This is just the same warmed over garbage that every 'New Age' person tells you. I don't think this really is helpful to me or to anyone else," I thought to myself. "This is really a waste of my time, being at this stupid class."

✸ Meeting Chang Again

Then something happened that would change my mind about Debbie and ultimately change my life as well. As she ended her discussion of chakras, Debbie put the group into a hypnotic trance, and proceeded to lead us in a guided meditation.

We were told that we were on a grassy hill, with a long narrow stairway in front of us. We were to follow her commands to climb down the ten steps of the stairway to a beautiful valley below. The valley I saw was full of colorful flowers and had a beautiful blue stream flowing down the middle of it. Along the river was a cobblestone path. I

followed this path to a beautiful pond with a large shimmering waterfall splashing into it. It was there that I saw Chang again. This was
the first time I had seen him in over two years.

"It's nice to see you again," I said timidly. "So what's going on
here?"

Chang looked at me patiently, and said, "You probably know
by now that there is no such thing as a coincidence. You have been
brought here tonight for a reason. I have a gift to show you. Are you
ready to receive your gift?"

I felt a chill run through my body. I really had not expected to see
Chang again, let alone at our angel class. "What kind of gift is it?" I
asked shyly.

"I bring to you tonight the gift of abundance," Chang announced.

I now felt as if I had entered an electrical grid of some kind. I felt
myself start to shake. All at once everything in my vision turned pitch
black, blacker than the darkest night I had ever known. In the distance I saw what appeared to be a bright glowing star coming toward
me. It was the brightest object I had ever seen. It appeared to glow a
thousand times brighter than the sun. The object came to rest in the
sky above my head. It seemed to glimmer and spin. As I looked at
it more closely, I noticed that it had thousands of long bright spikes
coming out of it.

At that point, Chang appeared to me again. "Keith, do you see this
star? It is your vision of abundance. Abundance is here for you. You
just have to accept it."

"Oh, this is really cruel, Chang. What kind of abundance are you
sending me anyway? Is it an abundance of cats or something?" I
asked sarcastically.

Seeming somewhat annoyed, but ever patient with me, Chang
continued, "Within ninety days you will find abundance."

I was unconvinced. "What kind of abundance are you talking
about? Maybe where you're standing things don't look that bad, but

my situation here really seems hopeless. My country has just gone to war, the economy of my city has gone to hell, no one is traveling so we have no tourist trade, and no one cares about angels or the art we sell. So where is this abundance of yours going to come from, anyway?"

"Keith, you can't keep putting all of this negativity out into the universe. There's always hope and there's always abundance. You just have to open yourself to accept it." Then Chang reached down and picked up handfuls of dollar bills. He pointed behind him and I saw mountains of dollar bills. "You have nothing to fear now, and you have nothing to fear in the future. Everything is going to be fine."

"Chang, I appreciate your good wishes and concern, but it's just that I really don't think all this abundance crap you're giving me is realistic. Things have just gotten too bad. I know that I'm probably just depressed to the point of hallucinating all of this. Maybe it's just my wishful thinking," I said to him, trying to rationalize my vision.

When Debbie brought the class back from our hypnotic trance, we all shared our experiences. Class members were impressed by my vision. I made a point of telling them that I really did not think it was real, and that it was probably not realistic to believe that anything was going to happen at all. The class finally ended and everyone left, satisfied with what they had learned that evening. But I felt I had wasted my time and that the messages that I had received were illusionary and unrealistic.

The next morning, I went over our financial records again. Things were even worse that I had thought. I had less than a week to save our store. I had already exhausted all of our resources. All of our credit cards were tapped out, and we only had $135 in our accounts. Our debts were over $5,000.

Store sales were less than $100 per day, which would not even pay for the rent, telephone, and electric bills. It all seemed very hopeless. I knew that if nothing else, the State of California would lock our doors for sure when we failed to pay our sales tax revenues on March 30th.

❀ A Vision in Bermuda

Saturday morning, March 15th, I received a phone call out of the blue, from a man who said he was at Los Angeles International Airport. "How do I get to your store from LAX?" he asked.

I gave him the directions and hung up the phone. At first I did not think anything of it, but then I thought to myself, "We get calls for directions to our store all the time, though LAX does seem funny. I wonder who is coming to see us from the airport."

About an hour later, a husband and wife who appeared to be in their mid-twenties arrived at our store. The couple wore very casual clothing and did not strike me as high-end customers.

The young man came up to me and said, "I'm the person who called you from LAX. Thanks for your directions, they were excellent."

I told him I was glad my directions were helpful, and asked where he was coming from.

The young man smiled and said, "We flew in today from the island of Bermuda in the Caribbean. I'm glad we found you."

I then looked at the young couple and asked, "So are you on vacation in California?"

They both looked at me and shook their heads, "No."

"So you're here on business then!"

They both shook their heads again, "No."

The man then spoke up: "We've come from Bermuda to visit your store. We want to see the art you have by the world famous angel artist Andy Lakey. Do you have this art here?"

"Oh, ye-yes we do," I stuttered, "It's in the gallery at the back of our store. Follow me."

We walked into the gallery, and they were astonished to see the large collection of spectacular paintings by Andy Lakey. I tried to act confident. I did not tell them that we had not sold a single painting from this gallery in more than six months.

I asked them where they'd heard about our store and Andy Lakey's art.

The young man took a deep breath and began to speak, "Well, we had never heard of your store or Andy Lakey's art until last week."

Again, I asked him where.

He looked at the woman with him and stammered, "Well, um, we really didn't hear about you, or the art."

"What are you trying to say?"

The man continued, shyly: "You see, we were doing a guided meditation last week in Bermuda and this angel symbol appeared to me. I didn't know what to make of it at first. I'd never seen anything like it before. So we went on the internet and looked up angels. There we found your store's Website and we saw the art of Andy Lakey for the first time. I knew this was a sign to me that I had to purchase a piece of this art. We booked a flight to LAX the next day, and here we are. Does this seem strange to you?"

I was so stunned by what I had been told that I just stared blankly at the couple, shook my head and said, "No. Stranger things than this have happened here before."

I began to show the couple the art. They were young, and I really did not think they could afford much. I pointed out two of my less expensive pieces and said, "This painting is $300 and this painting is $500."

The man looked across the gallery toward a fairly large painting of three golden angels. "How much is that painting?" he asked.

"Oh, that's $5,000," I said halfheartedly.

The young man reached into his wallet and pulled out a credit card, "Do you take American Express?"

Surprised, I nodded my head.

"Can you ship that painting to Bermuda?"

"Of course I can."

The young couple walked to the front of the store, where I ran their credit card, which was accepted without any problems. I shipped the painting on Monday, and a week later it arrived in Bermuda. The young man called me when he received the painting, to tell me that he and his wife were thrilled with it.

Just as Chang had foretold, abundance had come to me. The $5,000 paid off the store's rent and our state sales taxes. We were not out of the woods yet, but more was yet to come.

❀ A Lost Couple from Japan

About a month later, our store was open about an hour later than usual on a Sunday evening—a rare event for us. We had a customer who just wanted to talk and talk and not buy anything. We listened patiently and were about to gently insist that we had to close for the evening, when something amazing and life altering occurred.

As I looked out the doorway, I saw a car park directly across the street from us. This usually would not be an odd occurrence, except that the street was empty that night and there was no one else parked on the road at all. As I continued to stare at the car, an Asian man and woman, who appeared to be in their early sixties, walked across the street toward the store. They were both tall and thin and wore navy blue blazers like all the Japanese people I had met before. They looked much too elegantly dressed for our casual city.

The man came up to me and said, "I'm sorry to bother you, but we were at a conference in Santa Barbara today, and coming back on the freeway we accidentally got off on the wrong exit. Can you tell me how to get back on the 101 Freeway going south?"

I looked at the prosperous-looking couple, and after giving them the simple directions they needed, said, "You know what? I think you were diverted here for a reason. Since you're both here anyway, you should see our store."

The couple were too embarrassed to say no. I showed them all of our angel statues and knickknacks, before taking them to the gallery at the back. As we discussed the art, which seemed to impress them, I showed them the book I had written about it, *Andy Lakey's Psychomanteum*.

"Is this book for sale here?" the man asked.

"Yes," I replied

"If I buy a copy of your book will you sign it for me?"

"Of course I will," I answered.

The man then took a copy of my book off the shelf and asked me to sign it to him and his wife. I thought nothing more of this encounter at first. Then, about a week later, I received a call from a young woman named Nansuko.

"I'm calling about the book *Andy Lakey's Psychomanteum*," she said.

"Would you like to purchase a copy?" I asked.

"No, no," she replied, "I would like to speak to Keith Richardson about the book."

I introduced myself, and asked why she was calling.

"Well, Keith," she continued, "Do you know who that Japanese couple were, who came to your store about a week ago asking you for directions?"

"No," I answered, feeling a little confused.

"Mr. and Mrs. Kumeta are the most respected translators of spiritual books in the country of Japan. They read your book and were very impressed. They've asked me to translate it for them."

I was shocked and flattered at the same time. I cleared my throat and said, "I am very honored by your offer, but my book has already been translated into Japanese." I gave her Hanna's phone number and e-mail address so she could contact her.

A few days later, Hanna called me. She was very excited.

"Keith, I have some really great news," she said. "I told Mr. Matashima, the new president of JMA, about your book and the interest the Kumeta's have in it. He says that JMA wants to publish your book now."

"How does Mr. Matashima plan to publish my book?" I asked.

"Mr. Matashima has just purchased a major Japanese book company called Shinsensha Publishing. I heard about this because he hired me to translate Doreen Virtue's Angel Card decks for them a couple of months ago. This is a really great opportunity for both of us," she said.

I agreed to let Shinsensha publish my book, and a week later received a contract from Japan. I signed the contract on April 23, 2003, and the book was released in Japan on July 1—just under ninety days after I received the message of abundance from Chang.

My book immediately became a Japanese spiritual bestseller. With this success, we began to receive tens of thousands of dollars in orders for art and jewelry from Japan.

❀ ABC's *Good Morning America*

What happened with my book would have been a miracle in itself, but even more was about to happen. In August of 2003, I received a rather frantic call from a man asking to speak to Andy Lakey. But Andy is moderately famous, and values his privacy. I generally try to take care of the calls for him myself.

The male voice on the other end of the line was insistent. "I need to talk to Andy Lakey! I need to speak to him right now!"

"I sell Andy Lakey's art in my store, but I really don't know him that well," I lied.

"This is Brian O'Keefe. I'm the Producer of ABC's *Good Morning America* news program. We want to do a segment about Andy Lakey and his art. The show's host Diane Sawyer has asked that I make this happen right away. I need to speak to Andy Lakey and I need to speak to him right now!" the man persisted.

"Oops!" I thought to myself. I had lied to the wrong person. I quickly composed myself. "Give me your phone number and I'll see what I can do."

I called Andy Lakey as soon as I hung up the phone. Andy was excited by the opportunity to appear on this national news program, and called Mr. O'Keefe back right away.

We filmed much of the segment of *Good Morning America* at our store in September 2003. It aired throughout the United States and Canada a month later. This added publicity brought even more abundance to our business. We went from our worst holiday season in 2002 to our best holiday season in 2003.

In December that year, Andy Lakey and I were invited to do a major art show and book signing in Tokyo by JMA. This event was a great success and brought even more abundance to my life.

✿ Fox TV's "Miracles in the Making"

Finally, in January of 2004, I was contacted by Dan Schwab, the news director of the Fox television affiliate in Miami, Florida. Mr. Schwab told me that he had read my book and wanted to do a syndicated news segment about it for Fox affiliates across the United States. I agreed to let him film the segment in my store and two weeks later he sent a film crew all the way from Miami to do the shoot.

The news segment, titled "Miracles in the Making," featured our store and also a brief interview with singer Gloria Estefan. It was highly acclaimed and even considered for an Emmy.

Once the program aired, in February of 2004, we began receiving numerous phone calls from people wishing to purchase art and angels. New customers flew across the country to see our store and the gallery. We were also flooded with orders on our Website.

CHAPTER FOUR

Learning to Talk to Chang

BETWEEN 2003 AND 2004, DEBBIE taught three six-week angel courses at our store. Francesca and I attended and helped facilitate all eighteen classes. Each time I attended these classes, I became better at meditating and receiving messages from Chang. Everyone in our classes always seemed impressed by my psychic abilities. They would come to me even after their classes had ended, so I could help them answer questions about their lives through doing meditations with Chang.

I was able to get to the point where I could bring myself into the hypnotic state that Debbie induced just by closing my eyes, visualizing a stairway, and counting down ten steps. I would then go on my own to the forest-lined trail to the pond near a waterfall where Chang would meet me.

❀ First Contact

My first communications with Chang were very cryptic. They were mainly gestures and symbols that were supposed to represent various things to me. Sometimes I could figure the symbols out; other times I could not make out the meaning at all. I tried to figure out the significance of such symbols as long winding roads, trees with crows in them, various numbers and letters, and many gestures and hand signals from Chang.

Chang began to tell me, over and over, in words and gestures, that I was "the Chosen One."

"What am I chosen for?" I asked.

Chang answered me with a cryptic statement: "You were chosen to bring the light to the world."

"What does that mean?" I asked.

"You'll find out in time," he replied.

During each class, the other participants and I would practice receiving messages from our spirit guides and asking our spirit guides to contact the guides of other people in the group to answer their questions. At first, we would verbally ask each other the questions.

I felt that this was too easy. We then started writing down the questions on pieces of paper and giving them to the person doing the reading, folded and unopened. I felt that this also opened us up to preconceived ideas about the person we were reading and made me question the validity of messages we received.

Finally, to make the process totally foolproof, we had the people in our classes write their questions on a piece of paper, fold them up, and put them in a basket. All members were then told to draw an unknown anonymous question from the basket and see if they could get the message from their spirit guides that answered the question on their slip of paper. To my great surprise, I found that the answers that Chang gave me were always correct.

❀ Love Lifts Us Up

The first time I did the blind reading in our class, I held the paper in my hand and meditated with it. Then I began to receive a song in my mind. It was a song from the 1980s that I really did not know very well. The words went something like, "Love lifts us up where we belong—where the mountain's high and the eagles cry." As I heard these lyrics, I visualized a long road with cars racing down it. I opened the folded piece of paper and read the question.

It said, "Where am I supposed to meet my 'soul mate'?"

"Whose question is this?" I asked.

Lynn, a tall woman in her late forties raised her hand shyly. "It's my question."

I was feeling puzzled and a little embarrassed when I asked her, "Does 'Love lift us up where we belong' or 'where the eagles cry on a mountain high' make any sense to you, Lynn?"

Lynn seemed to have been caught off guard by my reading. She thought for a moment and then gasped, "Oh wow! How would you know that?"

"Know what?" I asked, surprised at her apparent concern.

Lynn took a deep breath and then began to speak calmly, "My daughter and I moved to California from Montana two years ago. We lived in the highest mountain region of the state. There was an eagle sanctuary near our home. We drove here from Montana and we plan to go back there again next month for a visit."

"Do you have a soul mate in Montana?" I asked.

"I don't know," she said. "Maybe I'll find out when I go back there."

Lynn had not yet found her soul mate, and I felt that my message was about more than just visiting Montana. I felt that she had to go back there to live.

After this reading, I found that I could bring in pretty accurate messages for anyone who left me a message on a piece of folded paper. Unfortunately, most of the questions had to do with soul mates. Chang feels that much of this information is karmic, and all you can do is provide people with some direction about where they can go to find their lover, and how they can open their hearts to receive this love once they have identified it. It is really up to them to make everything work out.

I was less than impressed by my psychic talents, but Francesca was enthralled with my ability to contact Chang. She felt that I had a gift, and that I needed to practice doing meditative readings in order to become better at what I did.

To my embarrassment and great concern, Francesca began scheduling me to do sessions with strangers she would meet in our store. She said that she knew in her heart that I would only tell people the truth, for the glory of heaven and not to promote my own ego. She felt that I could help many people overcome their fear of death and thus live fuller, happier lives.

I agreed to do the readings for the people that Francesca chose, but reluctantly. I knew I was receiving messages from my spirit guide, but felt that those I received the messages for would blame me, not Chang, for the information I gave them.

We did not charge people for my readings. Instead, we told them that a karmic exchange was necessary, and we asked that they make a donation to a charity of their choice.

The following are some of the readings I did between 2003 and 2005.

❁ Doreen

It was about 3:00 PM on a Friday afternoon in October when Francesca, in her exuberance about my newly found psychic abilities, told a customer named Doreen about Chang. She explained how I could meditate and receive accurate messages from him.

"Could your husband do a reading with Chang for me?" asked Doreen.

"Of course he can," Francesca answered. I was with another customer in the back of the store when she said, "Keith, I was talking with the lady in the front of the store, and told her about Chang. She says that she wants a reading from you after we close the store. I told her you would."

I was very unhappy about being put on the spot. We didn't even know this lady.

"I thought this would be good practice for you in getting messages from Chang," said Francesca, who appeared a little hurt by my anger.

"Okay, I'll do the reading," I said, "But please don't promise anyone else that I'll contact Chang for them without talking to me first."

Francesca promised, insisting she had only been trying to help me.

Doreen returned to the store about 6:00 PM. She seemed friendly, but acted like she was really too high class for me. The first thing she told me was, "I've gone to a lot of psychics and they all tell me the same thing. I want to confirm that your guide's readings are real, so I'm going to ask you the same question I have asked the other psychics and see if he gets it right."

I was uneasy enough about doing this "free" reading, without this woman trying to test my psychic abilities as well.

"What's your question?" I asked curtly.

"Well, my husband died five years ago, and I want to know if he is with me now?"

I meditated, and saw Chang. "Sorry to bother you," I said, "But Francesca set me up to do this reading for this lady. She wants to know about her husband who died five years ago. Can you tell me anything?"

Chang looked at me sternly and shook his head. Then he began to communicate with me using a series of gestures and symbols. This would have been confusing enough, without this pushy woman sitting in front of me with a condescending look on her face. My task was nearly impossible.

Chang showed me a road going up to a steep hilltop. On the hilltop was a tree with crows in it. I was very confused by these symbols, and asked him what they meant.

Chang just shook his head and gave me a blank look. He then showed me Doreen's husband. He looked happy and serene. He seemed to be doing okay on the other side.

"Are you with Doreen in the earthly realm?" I asked.

The man nodded, "Yes."

"Are you happy on the other side?" I asked.

The man nodded again.

I then faced the difficult task of trying to convey Chang's and the husband's messages to Doreen.

"I saw a road going up to a hill, with a tree at the end of it. The tree has two crows in it. Does this mean anything to you?" I asked.

"What you're telling me is vague and ridiculous. I've gone to a lot of psychics before, but you are definitely the worst I've ever met with." she continued, "This message doesn't mean anything to me."

I was now humiliated and embarrassed. "I also saw your husband during my meditation," I said shyly.

"What did he tell you?" Doreen demanded.

"He really didn't tell me anything," I said, feeling really stupid. "He just nodded his head yes to my questions about being with you here and about being happy on the other side."

"That's what all the psychics tell me, but the good ones tell me more details and they tell it much better than you do. You really need to practice doing readings," she said, rudely. "Does your 'Chang' have anything else to tell me?"

I meditated once more. "Chang, do you have anything that can help validate the information that I just gave to this woman?"

I immediately saw him in front of me. He smiled this time and spoke to me, for the first time ever.

"Keith," he said, "tell this woman that I have two affirmations for her. First let her know that the financial problems that California is now suffering will soon be helped."

He showed me mountains of money and said. "Your state will receive billions of dollars within the next two weeks. The second affirmation is that something significant will happen that will end the war in Iraq within the next thirty days."

I gave Doreen these affirmation messages from Chang. She just laughed at me. "Keith, I'm really glad that I didn't pay for this. This is a total waste of my time. Those were the most ridiculous affirmations I've ever heard and this is the worst reading that I've received in my life."

I was embarrassed and hurt by my experience with Doreen. "Maybe this whole Chang thing is all in my imagination. Maybe I'm just overworked or getting psychotic in my old age," I thought.

Two weeks later I changed my mind about Chang's messages. Major wildfires hit the mountains of Ventura and Los Angeles Counties. These fires were the most devastating and financially disastrous in California's history. After these fires, Southern California was declared a federal disaster area and received billions of dollars in federal aid to clean up the affected areas, rebuild the houses, and replace the watershed that was destroyed.

Thirty days later, Sadam Hussein was captured—a major event in the Iraqi war that eventually led to the beginning of a democratic process for that troubled nation.

I have done many readings since that time and everything has always been correct and the affirmations have always come true. I have learned not to question Chang's messages.

✸ Sally

By November of 2003, I was still gun shy about doing readings for our customers. I was amazed by the way that Chang had foretold the California wildfires and the capture of Saddam Hussein, but I was not ready to put my head on the chopping block again.

In mid-November, a deathly thin looking woman with short gray/black hair came to our store. Her name was Sally, and she had attended one of our angel classes. I gave her a hug when I saw her and asked her how she had been.

"I've been very depressed," she said. "That's why I've come here today."

"What's the matter?" I asked.

"My life has really got me down. Nothing seems to be going right for me, and I am considering suicide. I remembered how good you were at contacting your spirit guide in our angel classes. I need you to contact Chang for me. Can you do it?" she pleaded.

I really did not want to do any more readings after my humiliating experience with Doreen, but Sally seemed so desperate for answers. "Maybe Chang's words could save her life," I thought.

I agreed to do the reading, and explained that I did not charge. Relieved, she thanked me for my kindness, and I asked her to return after closing time.

Sally, Francesca, and I went into the art gallery, and Sally gave me a folded piece of paper with her question on it, as we did in our angel classes. I dimmed the lights and we sat down on chairs. I did my meditation and soon met Chang.

"Chang, this woman is very depressed. I really don't know exactly what her problem is. She wrote it on a piece of paper, and I haven't looked at it. Could you contact her spirit guide and see if he can get me a message that will bring her comfort?" I asked.

Chang nodded to me in approval and I received a message. "The woman's depression is caused by the loss of a loved one. Let her know that he's happy on the other side. Let her know that he's concerned for her, too."

"Can you give me something a little more substantial?" I asked. "This woman is really depressed, and I think she needs a sign."

Chang smiled at me, and then gave me a sign to validate this message. He put both of his hands together and formed the letter "M." "She will know what this means," he assured me.

I came out of my meditation and relayed Chang's messages to Sally. "Let me know if this means anything to you?" I asked. "Chang told me that your loved one is happy on the other side."

Sally began to cry. "Oh, that is the answer to my question," she said. "Look at the paper and you'll see."

I opened the paper, and saw that it read, "Is my son happy on the other side?"

"Chang also showed me the sign of an 'M.' He told me you would know what this means," I added.

Tears began to run down Sally's face now. "Oh, my God, it is my son," she said. "My son's name was Mark. He committed suicide last year. Everyone says you go to hell when you commit suicide. I'm so happy to hear that he's all right on the other side."

Sally left, grateful for the gift of comfort Chang had given her. I left with renewed confidence that I really could receive messages, and that these messages were real and meaningful.

❀ Ann

Ann is a spiritual counselor who has an office in Thousand Oaks, California. We had known her for two years, and had encouraged and promoted her work. In December of 2003, she asked me to contact Chang so she could receive some guidance about a very difficult client.

"Keith, I really don't know what to do," she said. "This client has attempted suicide before, and is now talking about it again. Please ask Chang what I should do!"

I meditated and met Chang. He looked at me a little inquisitively. "It's nice to see you again, Keith. Is there something I can do for you?"

"Chang," I said, "Ann has come to me with a problem, and she'd like your advice. Can you help me?"

"So, what's her problem?" asked Chang.

I explained about Ann's suicidal client.

Chang looked at me and shook his head, then replied, "There are many types of suicide. Some are noble and some are very cowardly. People who have cowardly suicides do so out of fear. They hurt others and they don't fulfill their life paths. The results of this form of suicide are really bad from a karmic point of view."

"What about the noble type of suicide?" I asked.

"This is a very good form of suicide," said Chang. "This is done when one gives his life for the good of others. Sometimes this is done in times of war. Other times it is done to give a noble example. Isn't your religion based on a suicide of this type?"

I was shocked by Chang's statement. It really caught me off guard. I had never thought of the heroic act of Christ as suicide before. Besides, how would a man from ancient Asia know anything about Christianity? Maybe this was another clue to Chang's identity.

"What about Ann's client?" I asked.

"Her client is threatening a very negative form of suicide," said Chang. "He is using these threats to control others. Tell her not to be taken in by his threats. It is his path to walk."

I gave Chang's message to Ann and she later told me that this approach was helpful in aiding her with her client.

❀ A Prediction of an Earthquake

In July of 2004, Francesca and I met a group of our friends for dinner. After dinner, our friend Rosie, a Hispanic woman in her early fifties, asked if I would talk to Chang for her. She said that she had a question for him.

I asked her what her question was.

She looked at me shyly. "I was watching the *Montel Show* this afternoon and the psychic Sylvia Browne made a prediction. I'm really concerned about it, and I want Chang to tell me if it's true or not."

"Don't tell me what the prediction was," I said. "I want to make sure that you and I both know that this is Chang's prediction, and not mine."

We dimmed the lights and I quickly went into meditation. In a moment I was with Chang.

"Do you know anything about the prediction that the psychic Sylvia Browne made today on television?" I asked.

Everything in my vision began to shake. I saw the trees moving back and forth and the water in the stream wash over its banks. "It's an earthquake," said Chang. "It will hit within ninety days. It will be a big quake, but don't worry. You're protected. You'll feel it, but it won't hurt, and it won't break anything in your store."

Rosie and the others at the dinner were amazed when I told them.

"That was exactly what Sylvia Browne talked about. She said that there is going to be a major earthquake in the next three months in Southern California," said Rosie.

The next week, Ron, a writer from *People* magazine, visited our store. I had met Ron through a class in screenwriting that I had taken at Ventura Community College in the spring. In the course of our conversation, he told me that he was writing a book about "spirit guides." I told him about Chang, and the prediction I had just received from him about an earthquake.

"Wow! That's amazing," said Ron. "Have you heard about the earthquake study they're doing at USC?"

"No. What are they saying?" I asked.

"They're saying that there's going to be an earthquake in Southern California by October. They think its going to be a 6.0 or higher on the Richter scale and will hit down toward San Diego." On September 29, 2004, the earthquake hit, exactly eighty-nine days after Chang's prediction. It was not where the scientists said it would be, three hours drive south of Ventura. Instead, it was about three hours north of us, in Parkfield, California. It was 6.0 on the Richter scale. We felt the quake, but we were not hurt by it and nothing in our store was damaged.

❀ Wanda

One afternoon in July of 2004, our friend Wanda came to the store, seeming anxious and a little nervous about something.

"What's the matter?" I asked.

"I'm concerned about my son-in-law Jonathan. He's not working and he's spending too much money. He's been married to my daughter for over fifteen years and he just hasn't been able to get his act together. She just keeps supporting him," Wanda replied.

"What can I do for you?" I asked.

"You can contact Chang for me and see what he thinks I should do about Jonathan," she said.

The store was open and I was kind of distracted but I could see that Wanda was upset, so I tried to calm my mind and go into meditation. A moment later I saw Chang.

"What should Wanda do about Jonathan?" I asked.

Chang shook his head, looked at me sternly and said, "Danger!"

"What does that mean?" I asked.

Chang waved his hands back and forth across his chest and said, "Danger! Danger!"

I relayed Chang's message to Wanda, but I was concerned about its meaning. I knew Jonathan, he did not seem to be a violent person, but this message was very clear.

"Has Jonathan ever been physically abusive with your daughter?" I asked.

"He's threatened her before when he was drinking, to my knowledge he's never hurt her," said Wanda.

"I'm getting a pretty strong message. I think you should warn her," I said.

Two weeks later Wanda called me. She seemed very upset. When I asked her what had happened, she told me:

"It's Jonathan. He's dead. My daughter found him in their bathroom last night. They don't know what he died of. The coroner is doing an autopsy. They're going to let us know next week. Can Chang tell me what he died of?"

I told her I would try to see if I could contact Chang, and went into a meditation while on the phone.

When I asked my question, Chang looked at me sadly, shook his head. "Poison!"

I relayed this message to Wanda. She was skeptical.

The next week she called me because she had received the autopsy report. "He died of a drug overdose," she told me. "We found out that he's secretly been buying drugs behind my daughter's back for the past several years."

"See, Wanda, Chang was right," I said. "Drug abuse killed Jonathan. And I am certain that Jonathan's drug abuse put your daughter's life in danger."

❀ Nancy

In early October of 2004, Kristen, our son Kevin's girlfriend, came to see us with a problem. Kristen is usually a very bright and cheery person, but today she was sad and withdrawn.

Francesca sensed that something was wrong, so she approached her and asked what was the matter.

Kristen began to cry. "It's my mother. She's really sick. She went in for a cancer screening yesterday and the x-rays showed suspicious spots on her ovaries. The doctors think it might be cancer. If it is cancer and it has spread too far, they don't know how much longer she will live."

Kristen's mother, Nancy, is the dear friend of ours who had participated in the James Van Praagh show a year earlier. We continued to celebrate all of our holiday events with her and her family. The news of her illness hit Francesca and me hard. It was like a lead weight had been dropped on our heads.

"Keith, we've got to do something. We've got to see if Chang can help Nancy," Francesca pleaded.

"What can Chang do for her?" I asked.

"Chang is a master spirit guide, he has a lot of power," said Francesca. "I want you to talk to Chang and see if he can heal her from the other side."

"We've never done anything like this before," I said, "I don't know if it'll work."

Francesca called Nancy and told her what we planned to do. "I know that Chang can heal you," she said.

I was not so optimistic, "Why are you giving Nancy false hope? I don't think that Chang can do anything about cancer."

That night we went to see Nancy. I told her that I would do a meditation and talk to Chang. This way I could see what he could do for her. I was uneasy as it was, and then I found out something that really concerned me. Nancy's husband Ted wanted to sit in on the reading. Ted is a "no nonsense" veteran police officer, and I could see from his face that he thought what I was doing was pretty stupid.

We went into Ted and Nancy's parlor and all sat down on chairs. I closed my eyes and went into meditation. Soon I saw Chang.

"Chang, I am really concerned about Nancy. Is she going to be okay?" I asked.

"Keith, don't worry about Nancy. She is going to live to see her grandchildren grow up," said Chang.

"What about the cancer?" I said. "What can be done about that?"

Then I saw Chang do something I'd never seen him do before. He reached into our dimension and put his hands into Nancy. He pulled out what appeared to be centipedes and scorpions.

"What are you doing?" I asked.

"I am getting rid of the bad energy she has in her," he replied. "She's going to be fine now."

I told Nancy what Chang had done, and she asked, "If I don't have cancer, do I still need an operation?"

Chang smiled at me and said, "Tell Nancy that she still needs a hysterectomy, but she does not have cancer."

"Can you give me a validation for Nancy, about her cancer?" I questioned.

"Keith, you're always looking for validation. Why can't you just have faith?" Chang asked. "Tell her, if you wish, that there is going to be a comet within the next thirty days. It will be so bright that people will be able to see it with their naked eyes."

"I haven't heard of any comets scheduled to come near earth in the next month," I said.

"That's what I'm talking about Keith. Don't be so skeptical, just have a little faith."

Nancy went in for her operation the next week. The doctors were baffled by the absence of the spots on her ovaries that they had found just the week before. When I went to see Nancy at the hospital, she asked me to thank Chang for curing her cancer. Ted was there with her, and he thanked me for what I had done. He was amazed by what had happened.

When we returned home, I went into meditation and met with Chang.

"Thank you for healing our friend Nancy," I said when I saw him.

Chang smiled and said, "Keith, you've still got a lot to learn. I didn't heal Nancy. She healed herself. I just stopped her from accepting the negative energies that make us believe we are sick."

In late December, a comet named Machholz appeared as a bright light in the night sky. Machholz was supposed to be faint, and most people thought that it would only be visible with a telescope. For some reason, it became four times brighter than expected and was visible to the naked eye. Scientists were amazed by this comet's brilliance and dubbed this the Christmas Comet. Chang was right again.

CHAPTER FIVE

Spirit Guides

AFTER LEARNING THAT I HAD a spirit guide and doing readings with people who also had spirit guides, I decided to do some research and find out what exactly a spirit guide was. The biggest challenge in discussing this concept is one of semantics. What one person may call a guardian angel, another person may call a spirit guide. I have decided to stick with the term "spirit guide" in this book, as I feel that this term best describes Chang, the entity I continue to see and speak with.

⊛ Definition

The most accurate definition of a spirit guide that I have found is: A highly evolved spirit that has spent many lifetimes on earth and has grown so much in spiritual purity that they now work with one or more people to help them reach their own spiritual enlightenment. Spirit guides have learned all of their earthly lessons, and are now here to help those they serve to master their own lessons.

From what I have read on the subject, a spirit guide is sometimes an ancestor, or a person you knew in a past lifetime. You have chosen this guide to help you with your present life.

Your spirit guide assists you only if you ask for their help. They are nonjudgmental and understand that you may have to make some mistakes and experience painful consequences in order to learn important life lessons. Sadly, some people go through their entire lives without realizing that they have a spirit guide.

❀ Biblical References

While trying to learn more about spirit guides, I discovered that there are several Biblical examples. In Samuel 28-7; King Saul receives a message from an oracle about his spirit guide:

> *Then Saul said unto his servants "Seek me a woman that has a familiar spirit that I may go to her and enquire of her." And his servants said to him, "There is a woman that has a familiar spirit at Endor." Saul disguised himself and went to the woman who produced the spirit of Samuel.*

I also learned that Christians today prefer to use the term "guardian angel." This term refers to an angel who helps people to use their free will correctly, allowing those they serve to make life choices that will lead them to heaven. The Bible refers to the work that guardian angels do in Psalms 91:11-12:

> *For he will tell His angels to care for you and keep you in all your ways. They will hold you up in their hands so your foot will not hit against a stone. You will walk upon the lion and the snake. You will crush the lion and the snake.*

❀ Ancient Beliefs

The Bible is not the only place where religions embrace spirit guides. The belief goes back as far as people have lived on earth, and possibly beyond. The earliest indications of spirit guides can be seen in the Cro-Magnon cave paintings in France. These paintings have been estimated to be from as far back in time as 30,000 BC, and indicate the presence of human and animal spirit helpers.

The oldest written records that refer to spirit guides have been found in Iraq. These writings were left by the Sumerians, who lived there about 3000 BC. The Sumerians believed that the spirits of their ancestors guided the living. They felt that each person had a spiritual entity that guided his or her life. Many alters to spirit guides have been found in the archeological excavations of ancient Sumerian homes.

The spirit guide beliefs of the Sumerians were later incorporated into the religion of the Semitic tribes who conquered the Sumerians around 1900 BC. These concepts were also included in Zoroastrianism, Judaism, and Egyptian religions.

In 1500 BC, the concept of the spirit guide Mithras arose. This belief traveled with the Indo-European people as they ranged from India to Great Britain. Mithras was believed to be a light-giver who brought love to all who followed him—a mediator between heaven and earth. The word Mithras means both "sun" and "best friend." According to my research, this belief system remained in existence up until the time of Christ.

❀ Meeting Spirit Guides

There are several ways that people meet spirit guides. I find my guides through guided meditations. Francesca often meets her guides in dreams. I have heard some people claim that they have seen their guides as actual earthly entities, during times of stress or emergency. Some even tell me that they see their guides at very spiritual moments in their lives, including times of healing, life crisis, or near-death experiences. Some easy ways to meet your spirit guides include listening to recordings of guided meditations like I did. John Edward, Sylvia Browne, and Doreen Virtue have excellent CDs that provide these meditations. You may also seek out a licensed hypnotherapist to give you a one-on-one session to help you encounter your spirit guide. Finally you can do silent prayer or meditation before going to bed and ask to meet your spirit guides in your dreams. This can work, too.

While reading about spirit guides, it became clear to me that they are very similar to the archangels described in the ancient religion of Zoroastrianism. These angels include "The Archangel of Good Thought," "The Archangel of Right," "The Archangel of Dominion," "The Archangel of Piety," "The Archangel of Prosperity," and "The Archangel of Immorality." These Archangels were the prototypes for the angels in Judaism, Christianity, and Islam.

Like the archangels of Zoroastrianism, each guide has his or her own specific abilities, and they all come to people when the guide's special assistance is needed. Over the past several years, I have been introduced to numerous spirit guides while doing my meditations with Chang. Each guide appears to have a specific duty that fits within the current needs of those they serve. The following are the most common guides I have communicated with.

❀ The Protector Guide

The Protector Guides' main responsibility is keeping humans out of trouble. They act like the traditional "guardian angel," capable of mentally warning people of danger before they experience it, keeping them from unintentional bodily harm. A study done on this phenomenon showed that 90 percent of people throughout the world who described a Protector Guide saw a Native American. I see Protector Guides in many of the readings that I do.

One very unusual experience comes to mind. It occurred last year, while doing a reading for a woman with an abusive husband. As I was speaking to Chang, I saw two Native Americans who appeared to be warriors. Their faces had painted stripes on each cheek. They wore headdresses that flowed to the ground with feathers. Each warrior had a bow and a quiver of arrows. When I asked Chang about the woman's husband, the warriors began shooting arrows at Chang and me. "What's going on here?" I asked.

"Those are this woman's Protector Guides," he said. "They are protecting her from you."

"Why are they protecting her from me? I'm trying to help her."

"Keith," said Chang, "this woman isn't ready to be helped yet. That's why the warriors are shooting at us. Tell her that you cannot help her until she can work out her feelings better."

I told the woman what Chang said and she agreed that she was not ready to do anything about her husband yet. She feared him, but she also feared leaving him. I told her that I could do nothing for her until she was ready to be helped.

❁ The Doctor Guide

Watching over our physical and mental wellbeing are the Doctor Guides. They are said to work with our other guides to help us overcome illness and mental health disorders. Some believe that Doctor Guides are the spirits of doctors who once lived on earth, and have now been chosen to work as healers from the other side. Chang has shown me doctor guides for many people that I have done readings for. Whenever I see one of these guides, I always ask the person about their health.

About 90 percent of the time, I find that they have recently been diagnosed with some sort of terminal illness. About 10 percent of the time, however, I find that the person I am reading is facing a very emotional issue that almost always has to do with a failing marriage.

Francesca met a French Doctor Guide named Capps in a dream shortly after I met Chang. The second time she saw him, he invited her to his home for dinner. She went to his house and met his wife. He told Francesca that he was a medical doctor. It seemed strange to me when I learned about Doctor Guides that Francesca would have one. I hoped that she was not sick.

Later I asked Chang about her Doctor Guide. He said, "The truth will set you free, you have true love, always cherish it." I conveyed this message to Francesca and she asked me what it meant. I told her that Chang was always giving me cryptic messages and it probably did not mean anything at all.

❀ The Gatekeeper Guide

The Gatekeeper Guides open doors to the spiritual realms. They also guard the doors to the other side, so only relevant guides may provide you with assistance. Francesca found a Christmas card with the name Nicole on it while walking a labyrinth at a local church. She felt that this was a message about our grandson Kyler, who was stillborn.

Francesca later had a dream about someone called Nicole. She came to her and said, "I will make sure that only the correct guides will come to protect you."

During a reading with Chang, we learned that Nicole was Francesca's Gatekeeper Guide. Francesca later realized that she needed a guide like this, because she is so open and sympathetic to other people's problems. Her Gatekeeper Guide works to keep her on track and grounded, so that she may help others without having them drain her spiritual energy in the process.

❀ The Joy Guide

The Joy Guides bring a sense of humor to those who need it. Their function is to lighten up the lives of those they serve through fun and laughter. The Joy Guides try to help you balance your work and play so that you will not get stressed out. Proverbs 17:22 states: "A Merry heart doeth good like medicine, but a broken spirit drieth the bones."

I have run into situations where I am certain that my Joy Guide is present. This often happens when I am leading a group meeting, either talking to Chang or speaking on various serious spiritual topics. Out of the blue, people begin to burst into laughter. I remember reading a transcript made from a recording of one of my group sessions and saying, "This group was out of control. I can't believe that these people didn't take me seriously."

I did not know it at the time, but I was just letting my ego get in the way of my spiritual understanding. My Joy Guide was trying to help me, and all those present, discover the ultimate truth that being spiritual is neither boring nor serious—it is fun.

Much new medical evidence is proving the old adage that "laughter is the best medicine." A study done in 1996 by Dr. Lee Burk and Dr. Stanley Tan showed that negative hormones were lower in participants that laughed rather than those who did not laugh. They found that laughter is a catalyst that releases negative emotions that cause negative chemical effects on the body. So listen to your Joy Guide, it is good for your health.

❀ The Relative Guide

The Relative Guides come very commonly to people who have recently lost close friends or loved ones. Most often, they appear as the spirit of a spouse or a parent. Their function is to help one through day-to-day life situations, and they may also be present at one's deathbed or during a near-death experience.

Chang often connects with Relative Guides when I am doing a reading of someone who has recently lost a loved one. This connection came very close to home when I did a reading for Francesca.

Shortly after our grandson Kyler died, after seven months in our daughter-in-law's womb, Francesca had me talk to Chang for her. She wanted to know why such a beautiful baby had to die, and why such a sad thing would happen to us.

Chang brought through my late mother, Marguerite: my Relative Guide. She was holding Kyler in her arms. I noticed that my mother, who had died a very painful lingering death several years earlier, looked great. She appeared to be in her early twenties and was healthy and beautiful again.

"Mom, why did Kyler have to die?" I asked.

"This was not the right time for Kyler to be born," she said. "Keith and Leah (our son and daughter-in-law) have a lot of things to accomplish first. Kyler will come back when the time is right."

The message was correct. After Keith's baby died, he and Leah were devastated. They sold their small home and moved back in with us. They saved their money and the four of us purchased a large beautiful home in Ventura together. Keith went on to earn his BA degree in Computer Technology from the University of Phoenix, and Leah was accepted by the Ventura School of Law and is on her way to earning her law degree.

Francesca and I would have many amazing things happen in our lives, too. Kyler's passing was an important part of the process that would put us both on our correct life paths. Chang has assured me that Kyler will come back to us, when we are all ready for him.

❀ The Master Teacher Guide

The Master Teacher Guides are the most agreed upon form of a spirit guide. These guides are self-realized, illuminated beings. Many of these entities lived as masters during their earthly existence, and continue to be masters in the spiritual realm.

The Master Teacher Guide is in charge of all other guides that enter a person's life. The purpose of this guide is to help people accomplish their purpose in this lifetime. The Master Teacher Guide brings people inspiration and guidance, and has access to knowledge of the past and the future. With the help of your Master Teacher Guide, you can overcome your karmic cycle of learning lessons life after life, and in time choose to stay in heaven forever.

This guide appears to you whenever you are ready to meet them. I feel that this is the best description for Chang, my Master Guide.

CHAPTER SIX

Finding Clues in Beijing

OUR NEWFOUND ABUNDANCE ENCOURAGED ME to continue to write my books. I completed my second book, *Doorways to Heaven*, in late 2003. I decided to do more research on the phenomenon called a "Psychomanteum" at one of its most documented locations: The Oracle of Delphi in Greece. Each of my books had discussed this occurrence, and I believed a new book with further research and documentation would be well received.

A Psychomanteum is an ancient name for a place where people in grief come in contact with the spirits of their lost loved ones. We had accidentally created a space like this several years earlier when we moved the spiritual paintings of Andy Lakey into our art gallery.

The concept of the Psychomanteum dates back many thousands of years. It is mentioned in Egyptian texts and in Homer's *Odyssey*. The most famous Psychomanteum is the Oracle of the Dead in Greece. For thousands of years this was used as a grief center for people throughout the Mediterranean. The site of this Oracle was found in the 1950s by Greek archaeologists.

Today, Psychomanteums are the subject of scientific study. Psychiatrist Dr. Raymond A. Moody has conducted extensive research and written numerous books and articles about this phenomenon. He has created working Psychomanteums at the University of Nevada, Las Vegas, and at his home in Alabama.

I began an extensive internet search of travel Websites that offered tours of Greece. The more I looked, the more discouraged I became. There just was not any type of travel itinerary that met my needs. The trips available were too long or too expensive. Then something happened that would change my life forever. I clicked the wrong link on one of the travel websites I was looking at, and a very interesting looking trip popped up.

It was a seven-day trip to Beijing, China, that included airfare, hotel, and some tours and meals. The price was just a little over $700 per person. It looked like a great deal and somehow the idea of a trip to China intrigued me. I call Francesca into my office.

Francesca looked at my computer screen, mesmerized. "This is really weird," she said. "Last night I had a dream I was in some sort of Chinese palace watching Chinese women dancers perform. They were all dressed in beautiful costumes. I wondered what this dream was supposed to be telling me, and now you show me this. I think for some reason we are supposed to go to China. I feel that this is a path we need to walk. Everything that has happened to us this year has been leading up to this. I think it has something to do with Chang."

I agreed that something very strange and wonderful was happening in our lives. "Maybe this is a sign," I said. "Maybe we will learn something more about our mission when we go to China."

I booked our trip for March 13, 2004.

❀ A Past-Life Regression

In February 2004, Debbie announced that she would no longer teach angel classes at our store when our current session ended in March. She was in the process of forming a psychic hotline service, and felt that she no longer had time to prepare and run our classes. We were sad to see her go, but we felt that she had fulfilled her purpose of bringing Chang into our lives and it was the right time for all of us to follow our own paths.

The final angel class was held the first week of March 2004, just one week prior to the trip we had booked to Beijing. As a going-away present to the group, Debbie did something she had never done. She performed a past-life regression with all of us.

I was never a big believer in past lives. They were just not part of my cultural reality, never discussed in my home, school, or church as a child. The little I had learned of the concept was that it was an unusual tradition of the Hindu people of India. It was something we made fun of as children. The Hindu people starved because they could not eat the cows that were abundant in their villages. They did not eat the cows because they thought that they might be a reincarnated friend or relative.

In recent years I had become more open to the concept of past-life regression. I had done several regressions before, and had experienced what appeared to be visions of past lives. But none of these experiences would prepare me for what I was about to see that evening.

I took many deep breaths and went under the trance as directed by Debbie. I passed through a long bright tunnel and entered a doorway into a time I had lived in before in a past life. I found myself standing in a very humble room with a dirt floor. I was wearing a white robe and had straw sandals on my feet. In the corner of the room were two other people dressed like me, each were sitting holding bowls of noodles, which they were eating with chopsticks.

"What is the date here?" I asked.

A voice in my head said, "It's the mid-seventeenth century."

"Where am I?" I asked.

"You're in a place that you now call Beijing, China," the voice answered.

Finally, I asked, "How old am I here?"

"You are in your early twenties," the voice replied.

I walked across the room and looked closely at the two people who continued to eat their noodles. They were both men. They did not seem to know I was there. They both looked quite young, maybe in their early teens. I looked into their eyes and was surprised to realize that I knew both of them.

One of the young men was my friend Mary-Pat. She had worked at our store several years before, and we have remained close to her and her family. The other person was Andy Lakey. Andy had been creating art for our store for nearly ten years, and when I first met him back in 1995, I had had a strange feeling of recognition. This further confirmed my suspicion. Then a thought hit me like a bolt of lightning: "Maybe this has something to do with Chang. Maybe Chang was one of my family members in this lifetime."

I stood in front of the two people, looked both of them in the eyes and said, "Where's Chang?"

The two men stopped eating their noodles, shook their heads in unison, and said with little emotion, "Chang? Oh yes, Chang. He's in charge here." Then they casually resumed their meal.

"What does that mean?" I thought to myself. "What could Chang be in charge of here anyway?"

I left the crude dwelling, more confused than ever. I awoke from my meditation and shared my vision with the class. No one in our group knew what it meant either. I now had more questions and fewer answers than before. And Francesca and I were leaving for Beijing in less than a week.

❀ The Trip to Beijing

The long-awaited day of our departure finally came. Our flight was long and uneventful, including a two-hour layover in Tokyo. We arrived in Beijing about 5:00 PM, after traveling for over sixteen hours. At the gate, our tour guide Lee met us and the other members of our tour. Lee led us to our shuttle bus, and accompanied us to the Best Western Hotel located in the southeastern part of Beijing.

The next morning we awoke to see the bustling city of Beijing out of our hotel window. We were excited to begin our five-day whirl-wind tour of China.

The room we had was clean and spacious, with an elegant bath-room with a polished marble floor. I took my shower and managed to get water on the floor. Dressing in the bedroom a few minutes later, I heart a loud thump. Francesca had slipped on the slick marble floor and fallen on her face. I ran down the hall and got a bucket of ice, and she sobbed with pain as I placed an ice cold washcloth over her eye. Francesca would have a black eye for the rest of our stay in China. Once Francesca had recovered from her fall, we went down for breakfast, and then met up with Lee and other members of our tour for a bus to Tiananmen Square and the Imperial Palace.

❀ The Imperial Palace

Lee told us that Tiananmen Square was the largest city square in the world. It was over 100 acres. On entering, we found ourselves sur-rounded by a plague of aggressive street vendors attempting to sell us numerous patriotic Chinese souvenirs, including Mao Zedong wrist-watches, Chinese flags, and communist party caps of olive drab with red stars. The vendors screamed and haggled with members of our tour to negotiate prices. Lee warned us that some of the vendors were pickpockets. I felt someone reach into my back pants pocket at one point, but luckily I had my wallet in a pouch attached to my ankle.

After about a half an hour of being hounded by the vendors, we were at last escorted to the main gate of the Imperial Palace. Lee told us that the palace was completed in 1421, seventy-one years prior to Columbus's discovery of the New World. It took twenty years, and the work of over 200,000 laborers to complete it. For nearly 500 years, its moat-encircled 180 acres housed twenty-four emperors of the Ming and Qing Dynasties. Over 9,000 people lived in the palace at any time, including courtiers, servants, and retainers.

On entering the palace, we were struck by its enormity and grandeur. Everything appeared to be bigger than life. There were 9,999 rooms in all. Only the emperor had been allowed to have this many rooms in his house. Anyone else attempting to duplicate this number of rooms would have been executed.

As Francesca and I walked through this great palace we both felt a sense of déjà vu come over us.

"Do you feel it, Keith? There's something familiar about this place. I know I've been here before," said Francesca.

"I know exactly what you're talking about," I replied. "I'm tingling all over, too."

"Do you think we were here in a past life?" she asked.

"It doesn't look like the place I saw during my past-life regression in China," I said.

"I think I remember this place. I think I used to live here," whispered Francesca.

We moved pretty quickly through the vast palace as Lee herded us like cattle through it. I noticed that there were additional buildings on all sides of the ones that we were visiting, but our tour never stopped. We just kept marching onward. We made it to the end of the palace in a little over an hour, much too fast to see such a magnificent and sprawling structure.

❀ The Great Wall of China

The next day we traveled to the far northwestern part of Beijing to visit a rebuilt segment of the famous Great Wall of China. This is the part of the wall that is shown in movies, travel programs, and brochures. It is not old at all. It was rebuilt in the 1950s and is now one of China's best-known tourist attractions.

Lee brought us to the Badaling Wall, the most famous and most touristy segment. He told us that the Great Wall of China is the longest man-made structure on earth. It has been part of China's heritage for over 2,000 years.

There are two sides of the wall at Badaling that one can climb—an easy side and a more difficult side. Of course, Francesca and I picked the most difficult side. The wall we chose to climb was nearly vertical, making it appear nearly impossible to ascend. The hike reminded me a little of climbing the pyramids of Mexico. Parts of the wall were so steep that you had to pull yourself up using the handrails at the sides. Further adding to the difficulty of climbing the wall were the aggressive vendors that attacked tourists like a swarm of angry bees. They sold a large variety of Great Wall souvenirs, including plaques, tee shirts, and scarves. The vendors were happy to barter with you forever, and to chase you and haggle their way up the wall, if you showed even the slightest interest in any of their wares.

After nearly an hour of climbing and being constantly swarmed by vendors, Francesca and I came to the end of the segment of wall. It was worth the climb. Stretching out in front of us and into infinity were the ruins of the real wall. It was truly amazing: the largest physical human achievement I had ever seen.

✽ The Chang Tombs

After leaving The Great Wall of China, our tour headed for one of the Ming Tombs. We visited the Changling tomb, which Lee told us was the largest and best preserved of the Ming tombs. It contained the bodies of a fourteenth-century emperor named Zhu Di (pronounced like Judy) and his two empresses. Adjacent to this tomb was a vast offertory room. In the middle of this room was a large bronze statue of Zhu Di.

Francesca looked at the statue and said, "Keith, I think we have been led here. I think we've found Chang."

I looked at the statue of the Chinese emperor, then shook my head and said, "No, I don't think that's him. Chang had a goatee and a long mustache. He also had a ponytail. Zhu Di doesn't look like that at all. Zhu Di has a round, fat face. Chang had a narrow, thin face. I'm sure it's not him."

Then Francesca saw something that made her very excited. On the far wall of the offertory room was a chart of all of the Ming tombs. Above the chart was the inscription "Chang Tombs."

"Look Keith! We've found Chang," she said gleefully. "This is amazing. This is why we've been led to China. We've found your spirit guide."

Francesca found Lee and showed him the chart. "Which one of these tombs is Chang buried in?" she asked.

"There is no emperor named Chang," said Lee politely.

"Then why is his name on this chart?" Francesca asked.

"The word Chang is not the name of an emperor," Lee said patiently. "Chang is a title we bestow upon emperors. It means 'Son of Heaven.'"

When Lee said this, something clicked in my brain, "Oh, my God!" I thought to myself. This may be what my past-life regression was about. In my regression I had asked about Chang and was told that he was in charge here. "Chang is the word that the peasants use to address their emperor. Maybe I was involved with an emperor of China in the seventeenth century."

"Lee, are any of the Ming tombs from the seventeenth century?" I asked.

"No, the tombs from the seventeenth century are the Qing tombs. These tombs are far away from here, on the other side of Beijing. It's more than four hours drive from downtown Beijing," he said.

I asked him if there was a tour to the Qing tombs, but he said there was not. "You have to hire a driver or take a cab or bus. It's a long ride and I really don't recommend it," he said abruptly.

The tour of the tombs ended without further fanfare. We had seen many things and learned much about China, but we were still just as confused as before about what my encounter with Chang really meant, or even if someone named Chang ever really existed.

✿ The Temple of Heaven

The second day in Beijing, Francesca and I decided to take a guided tour of the Temple of Heaven. This temple contains one of the most famous buildings in China. If you have ever eaten in a Chinese restaurant there is a good chance you have seen a picture of this structure on your menu.

The Temple of Heaven was laid out and constructed during the time of the Ming Emperor Yongle (1406–1420). The entire temple complex includes a park, the "Hall of Prayer for Good Harvest," the "Circular Alter," the "Imperial Vault of Heaven," and the "Hall of Abstinence."

The Hall of Prayer for Good Harvest is the most famous building in this complex. It consists of a tall circular wooden hall with three blue tiled roofs, each capped with a golden ball. This building has become the symbol of imperial Chinese architecture. The hall stands 125 feet tall and 98 feet across.

The Temple of Heaven was once the most important temple in China. For over 500 years, during every winter solstice, the emperor led processions out of the Imperial Palace across Tiananmen Square and then southward down the imperial way to the Temple of Heaven. Here, he would perform rites and make sacrifices to the universe to insure good harvests for the people of China.

Before leaving for Beijing, my friend Barbie, a very active, high-spirited woman in her early nineties, called and asked me to say a prayer for her at this temple. She and her late husband, a reporter for United Press International, had visited the temple just after World War II. Barbie felt that it was one of the most spiritual places she had ever gone to. I was excited to experience this sacred shrine for myself.

The entrance to the temple complex was filled with hundreds of elderly Chinese people, all involved in various leisure activities.

Some were playing cards; others were playing musical instruments; others were singing.

"What are all these people doing here? Is this some sort of festival?" I asked Lee.

"No," he said. "These people are retired. They come here every day to get together and have fun."

"Wow, this temple really is important to the Chinese," I thought to myself.

But as we entered the temple complex, I discovered something that made me feel sad. This once important religious center had been turned into a cold, dispirited museum. I could not even say a prayer for Barbie. The entrance to the Hall of Prayer for Good Harvest was locked tight. Visitors were no longer allowed inside.

I was upset and disappointed by this and my other experiences with Chinese spiritual centers. I felt that the lack of faith, which the communist government had promoted, was robbing the Chinese people of their souls. I felt that these people were advancing economically, but were greatly lacking spiritually.

"Maybe this lack of spirituality in China is part of the reason that Chang has guided me to Beijing," I wondered.

❀ Learning to be Independent in China

During our last few days in China, Francesca and I learned to be self-sufficient. We met a Chinese-American woman named Irene from Pacific Palisades, California. Irene had been to China many times before, and spoke fluent Mandarin. Her husband was an international trade merchant, but, according to Irene, was not very adventurous. Irene loved going on excursions with Francesca and me. She said we were not afraid of anything. We ate everything, we went to see exotic sights, and considered every new day precious and exciting.

Irene proved to be a valuable asset to us, too. She knew how to explain to cab drivers where we wanted to go and she knew how to order food in Chinese. Irene's greatest asset was her ability to bargain with vendors at marketplaces. She knew what the real prices for goods were, and she knew how to get these prices from the vendors.

We visited the Russian Market, the Friendship Store, Silk Alley, the Pearl Market, and the Sunday Dirt Market with Irene in tow. We paid for all her cab fares and even invited her out for some meals. She thought we were really generous and kind to her, but we knew that she was worth her weight in gold to us.

With Irene's help, Francesca and I learned to overcome our fears of being on our own in China. We did not speak Chinese, and doubted that we could ever learn this very difficult language. We knew, though, that we could get by on our own anyway. Our experience with Irene showed us that we would never have to be confined to tourist destinations in China again.

❀ The Flight Home

It was a cold gray day when we boarded our flight back to the United States. Francesca and I had been amazed by the beauty of China, as well as the friendliness of its people. We were sad, however, that we had not discovered all that we needed to learn about Chang.

As we flew back to the United States, we discussed what we knew so far about Chang. We felt more and more that he was not an ethereal figment, but a real person who had lived in China in the past.

"When I first saw Chang several years ago, he looked Chinese," I said. "Then I had the past-life regression last week and got the message that he was with me in the seventeenth century. This week Lee told us that the word 'Chang' meant 'Son of Heaven' and that this term was used to address Chinese nobility."

"Was there anything else that could help us find out who Chang is?" asked Francesca.

"Yes," I said, "there was also that message that I received during the reading with Elizabeth that intrigued me. What could Chang have to do with Christianity? Why would he tell me that my religion was based on suicide? We've come a long way since I first saw him, but I don't know what else we can do to find who he is."

Our flight arrived in Los Angeles on time. We returned home and resumed work at our store, and told everyone we met of the wonderful time we had on our trip to China. But deep down inside we both felt emptiness. We could not get the questions about Chang out of our mind, and somehow we believed that we had failed to accomplish what we had set out to do on our trip to China.

CHAPTER SEVEN

The Butterfly Princess

TWO DAYS AFTER WE RETURNED to the United States, we invited a group of friends to our house. We shared our adventures in Beijing and showed them photos of our trip. When we were finished sharing our experiences, one of our friends suggested that I meditate with Chang and get messages for the group. Everyone was amazed by the accuracy of the answers Chang gave me. When I was done communicating with Chang for the group, we joined together to do a group guided meditation. I played a CD of Doreen Virtue's *Spirit Guide Meditation*, and nearly everyone in the group went into a trance.

I had become very in tune with meditation and talking to Chang as time went on. Francesca, on the other hand, just could not figure out the process of meditating. She would just lie down on the floor and close her eyes. Many times she would go to sleep. I became more and more annoyed with her lack of ability to concentrate on the directions from the CD.

This time, I did not follow the directions of the meditation either; instead I again met with Chang. "Chang, when will Francesca ever learn to meditate?" I said irately. "Will Francesca ever get it? She's not even trying anymore and it is starting to upset me. This is really distracting for me and everyone else here, too."

To my surprise, Chang looked at me sternly and responded, "Keith, why are you so upset with Francesca? Isn't she your 'true love'? True love is not an easy thing to find, you know. I never found true love during my lifetime. You must cherish and nourish your true love. True love is very karmic. It must be earned over many lifetimes. When you finally receive this gift, you must cherish it. Please don't mock it. Try to stop being so serious."

I was shocked by this message. I shared it with Francesca after our meeting. As I spoke to her, she began to cry.

"I think I know what this means," said Francesca between sobs. "I believe that we were connected somehow in China. I know this is a very important part of the puzzle."

The next week, Francesca and I went to Riverside County, about a three-hour drive from Ventura, to purchase artwork by Andy Lakey. We had been on the road for about an hour, when Francesca shouted, "I've got it! I've got it! I know who Chang is."

"So who's Chang?" I asked skeptically.

"Chang's my father," said Francesca.

"How can that be? I've known your father for years. He's Dr. Elmo Quesada from Nicaragua. His name isn't Chang," I said mockingly.

"No, no, Keith, don't make fun of me. This is really very serious," said Francesca. "I just got a premonition. In a past life in the seventeenth century, I was the daughter of an emperor who was known as Chang."

"How do you know you weren't his concubine?" I joked, still not taking her seriously.

"Keith, don't you remember what happened last week during our meditation?"

"No, refresh my memory," I said.

"Remember that you were upset that I had given up trying to meditate, and you asked Chang what you could do to get me to quiet my mind, so I would be able to participate with the rest of the group. Chang got mad at you, didn't he?" she said.

"Yes, he did," I replied, more timidly now. "He told me that you were my true love. He said that true love was something rare and beautiful, and that I should respect it."

"Who else would tell you something like that but my father?" stated Francesca emphatically. "Who else but my father would be so protective of me?"

"Everyone thinks that they were something special in their past lives," I said. "This is the kind of thing the phony crystal ball readers tell you about to keep you going back and paying them. Every phony psychic out there tells you that you were Cleopatra or Mary Magdalene, or maybe you swam with dolphins in Atlantis or something. For the most part, if you lived a past life, I'm sure it was a very simple one—not as a princess. That's just not the way the odds work out."

✾ Validation

Two nights later, when we returned home from work, Francesca asked me go into meditation to communicate with Chang. She wanted me to validate her intuition about being his daughter.

I closed my eyes and went into a meditative state. When I met Chang I asked him, "Was Francesca any relation to you in your life in the seventeenth century?"

To my shock, Chang replied, "Keith, I'm glad Francesca finally figured it out. I really was her father. That is why I am here, and that is why you are together in this lifetime. You both have a mission to accomplish."

"What is our mission?" I interrupted.

"Your mission is to work together to bring more peace and love to the world," he said. "Peace and love are the only truth, everything else is an illusion."

I relayed this message to Francesca and she was stunned by the news.

"I told you that I felt I was Chang's daughter," she said, beginning to sob. Tears pooled in her eyes as she came to the full realization of her past life in China, and of her mission in this lifetime.

"I believe in reincarnation, but I have never been prepared to receive a message like this one," she said.

❀ The Kangxi Emperor

The next morning, Francesca began researching seventeenth century Chinese Emperors. She found a copy of a *New York Times World Almanac* that we kept in our bathroom, and she began looking up the names of the emperors of the Qing Dynasty. The emperor's name she gave me was Shunzhi.

I looked him up on the internet and found that the picture that it showed for Shunzhi did not look anything like Chang. The next emperor's name she gave to me, however, was Kangxi.

"Look, this emperor has a 'K' name, just like you, our two sons, and your father. This must mean something," said Francesca excitedly.

"Let me look him up," I said skeptically.

I typed the name "Kangxi" into the computer, and was shocked by the portrait that came up. It was Chang, exactly as I continued to see him. He was wearing a long golden gown with dragons on it. He had a beard, a goatee, and a mustache that went down both sides of his mouth. On his head was a double-decker red hat with a blue brim.

"Francesca, look at this!" I shouted. "I've found Chang."

Francesca looked at the portrait on the screen of my computer, and again began to cry as she looked upon Chang's gentle face.

"I recognize him. I've known him for a long, long time. I know he's my father," she said.

❀ True Love's Vision

The next week we invited some friends to our home to do another meditation together. I played a CD about past lives by psychic Sylvia Browne this time. Again, I did not follow the meditation, instead meeting with Chang. As I began to speak with him, something really unusual happened. I saw the scene around me change abruptly. I was no longer by a lake with a waterfall. Instead I experienced something like a video clip running through my brain. Everything turned to vivid color as I watched a scene play out from early China. To my surprise, I saw myself in this vision, too.

I saw a beautiful Chinese princess, and for some reason felt a great love in my heart for her. I was shocked when I realized it was Francesca. She came to me and held me close to her. Chinese guards yanked her away from me, and put her into an elaborate Chinese-style sedan.

The sedan was ornate. It appeared to be covered with gold leaf that glistened in the sunlight. It was enclosed and had glass windows. The carriage was not pulled by animals, but instead had four wooden handles that came out from it. Four large Chinese men stood holding each handle.

When the princess was locked in the sedan, the four men began to quickly depart with it. I saw Francesca's face looking out of the window. She was crying. I cried too, as I sadly waved goodbye to my true love. I knew that we were never to meet again in that lifetime.

Once this scene had played out, Chang continued to talk to me. "Keith," he said, "you wished to experience true love once, but I couldn't let this happen. You were Chinese and she was Manchurian. It was my people's belief at the time that the Chinese people were an inferior race. We had just released them from slavery. It was forbidden for a Manchurian to marry a person of Chinese decent. It would have been a great scandal for the emperor's daughter to marry one. It broke my heart, it broke your heart, and it broke my little butterfly's heart too. I did it to save the empire. If you had married my daughter, it would have caused a great deal of turmoil. It might have cost me my position as emperor. As your guide in this life, I am going to repay my karmic debt to you, and make certain that your true love survives."

I really did not know what Chang was talking about. I was totally confused.

"How did you bring us together again in this lifetime?" I asked.

"It wasn't easy; it took five lifetimes of karmic lessons for you to figure it out. And it almost didn't happen for you again this lifetime," said Chang.

"What do you mean? Why would I turn true love down?" I asked.

❀ A Bad Marriage

"Your lifetime in China made such an impression on your soul that during each lifetime you had for the past 300 years, you have tried to obtain wealth and social status rather than true love. Didn't you do this in this lifetime, too?" Chang asked.

"Yes, I guess I did," I replied, reluctantly.

I remembered that just before I was discharged from the Navy, I met a young woman who personified all my qualifications. She came from a wealthy family. Her father was a prominent attorney from Los Angeles. Her mother was a socialite. She had big connections in the Los Angeles social scene. She knew and associated with movie stars and some of the top corporate figures of the 1970s.

"Did you find true love and happiness with her?" Chang asked.

"No. I married the young woman just a few weeks after I left the Navy and immediately found that she and her lifestyle made me completely miserable. She did, however, lead me to Francesca," I said.

"No, Keith, you're wrong," said Chang. "I led you to Francesca. I owed you a karmic debt. That's why I had to help you."

"What do you mean?" I asked.

❀ Meeting Francesca

"Think about what happened," said Chang. "You had been in your miserable marriage for about one year when you first met Francesca. She was your wife's best friend's husband's sister. You were invited over to their house to meet her the day after she arrived in the United States from Nicaragua. Her parents had sent her to attend school in the United States because they didn't like the man she planned to marry."

Chang asked me how I had felt when I first saw Francesca.

"I felt like I had always loved her," I replied. "I had never felt this way before. I thought at first that it might be because she seemed so exotic. I had never met a woman from Nicaragua before. She was sweet, wonderful, and beautiful. And she didn't speak a word of English. My Spanish was pretty bad then too, so we didn't communicate verbally, but I just felt a magnetic pull to her. It was like our souls were intertwined somehow."

"So what did you do to make your relationship with Francesca take place?" asked Chang.

"I didn't do anything. I felt that considering I was married and she was engaged, our situation was hopeless. I felt a secret passion for her, but I didn't act on it. It just wouldn't have been right."

"Keith, do you understand now how I was able to get you and Francesca together? It wasn't easy, you know. You probably thought it was all just a big weird coincidence, didn't you?" questioned Chang.

His words hit me like a bullet. "You were involved in that?" I asked, "You're telling me that you brought us together?"

"Think back on it," he said. "Remember what happened that night in March of 1974. You were attending California State University at Los Angeles, and you had gone that evening to take a class. You found that your instructor was ill and that the class had been cancelled. Rather than returning home, you decided to go upstairs to the coffee shop and see if any of your college friends were there. The building was quite tall, and had a series of moving stairs to take you to the top. That night the system was broken and you decided to do something that you had never done before. You pushed the button to take the elevator."

"Oh, that's right!" I interrupted. Taking that elevator was the event that changed my life. When the door opened I was amazed to see Francesca's sister-in-law Laurel standing alone inside. I had left my wife six months before, and was in the process of divorce. I never expected to see Laurel or Francesca again."

I asked Laurel what she was doing there. She said that she planned to attend a class that night, but it was cancelled and that she was about to leave for home. I invited her to come upstairs with me for a cup of coffee. She agreed, and we spent some time catching up on our friendship.

As Laurel prepared to leave, she said, "Keith, you have to come over for dinner sometime. I'm sure Rennie (her husband and Francesca's brother) would really be happy to see you again. We've really missed seeing you since you broke up with your ex-wife."

Laurel wrote her phone number on a piece of paper, and handed it to me. I took the paper and put it in my pocket.

I told Laurel I had hesitations about going to her house, as my ex-wife and I had broken up on really bad terms, and I was concerned that she might show up while I was there. I really didn't want to have to deal with her again.

"Don't worry about that," said Laurel. "We haven't seen your ex-wife since you two broke up. We think she somehow blames us for your break-up. The last time I spoke to her she was really rude."

I assured Laurel that our relationship ended due to the differences my wife and I had with each other, and that it had nothing to do with her or her husband. I told her I would call her sometime and set a date for all of us to get together again, but I really did not mean it. I felt that my relationship with them had ended when I broke up with my ex-wife.

Over the next month, I began to get a feeling that I should call Laurel and set up our dinner engagement. I don't know what made me feel that I needed to see these friends again, but the feeling became more and more compelling. There just seemed to be a voice screaming in my head constantly, telling me to make the call.

I finally broke down and called Laurel. The voice that answered, however, was the voice of a young woman with a strong Spanish accent. At first I thought I had gotten the wrong number.

"Who is this?" I asked.

"This is Panchita (Francesca's nickname)," the voice on the phone replied.

I was shocked and delighted to be talking to the young woman I had been so captivated with. I did not know what to say at first.

"I didn't know you spoke English," I said, still shaken.

"I've been going to school here for two years now and I've learned," she replied. "Are you going to come over and see us, Keith? We miss you."

"Of course I will," I stammered. She put Laurel on the line, and we set a date for the next Saturday.

I arrived right on time at the house but Laurel and Rennie were not home yet from work, and Francesca answered the door. She was as exotic and beautiful as I remembered.

"Why do I feel this way about this young woman?" I thought to myself. "I've known her for just about two years, but I've never really spoken to her face-to-face."

Francesca invited me into the house and brought me a soft drink. "Do you know how to play Chinese checkers?" she asked.

"Yes," I replied.

"Good," she said, and proceeded to pull a set of Chinese checkers out of a cupboard and put it on the table.

"Let's play," she said enthusiastically.

I always thought I was pretty good at Chinese checkers, but I was wrong. Francesca proceeded to trample on me like a heard of elephants, one game after another. It was beyond humiliation. It was complete devastation. Yet she was so sweet and beautiful that it did not rattle me.

"What a brilliant young woman. What a combination of beauty and brains," I thought.

"Where did you learn to play Chinese checkers like that?" I asked humbly.

"I don't know," Francesca replied. "I've always been good at this game, since I was a small child. No one has ever been able to beat me." Her kind words did not totally heal my bruised ego.

About a half hour after I got there, Laurel arrived, and I was spared further humiliation at the hands of Francesca. Laurel prepared dinner and told me that Rennie would be home soon. After he arrived, we all began to catch up on old times.

We ate dinner together and shared stories and jokes and remembered what really good friends we all were. After dinner, Laurel suggested that we go to a movie. I thought it sounded like a good idea, but Rennie said he had worked hard that day and just wanted to get to his bed and go to sleep.

He then suggested that Francesca and I go to the movie. My heart skipped a beat. To me, this was like a dream come true.

"Do you want to go to the movies with me, Panchita?" I asked shyly.

"Of course I would," she replied.

This was a totally wonderful turn of events. We went to see a very popular movie of the time called *The Sting*, starring Paul Newman and Robert Redford. I enjoyed the movie immensely, but Francesca had a difficult time understanding the 1930s slang in the film's dialogue. Now I was finally in control, as I explained much of the movie to her.

Before we said good-bye that evening I invited Francesca to go with me the next afternoon to see the roses at Descanso Gardens in La Crescenta, California. I told her they had a black rose growing there. I had gone there on a field trip with a biology class a few years earlier and remembered seeing these roses. Francesca was excited with the opportunity to see such a rare flower, and agreed to go. We started dating after this, and we were married the next year. We've now been together for over thirty years.

"Do you think this was all just a coincidence, Keith?" Chang asked, as I finished recounting the story.

"Before I met you, I did," I replied. "Now I see that there seems to be a karmic plan much bigger than me at work here. What is it that Francesca and I are supposed to do?"

"You're supposed to help bring the message of peace and love to the world," said Chang. "Everyone on earth has to learn that in heaven there is only one religion. This religion is love. They have to realize that we are all one. Love and peace are the only truths."

❀ My Name Means Butterfly

Upon learning of our relationship in the seventeenth century from Chang, Francesca became intrigued and somewhat obsessed with her role as a Chinese princess. She began to read everything available in English about China and the Qing Dynasty. She also learned the word for "Daddy" in Mandarin Chinese, which is "Baba," and she began to refer to Chang as her Baba.

At first this bothered me. It seemed sort of silly and disrespectful to Chang. Chang, however, told me that he did not mind Francesca using the term. In fact, he said that he liked it, though he did make it clear to me that he did not want anyone else calling him Baba, except for his little butterfly, by which he meant Francesca.

Francesca felt that the term Baba represented the love and respect she had for Chang. "He's my father," she said. "You always call your father 'daddy' or something like that, out of respect for who he is. I know that love never dies and my love for my Baba will always be with me."

Francesca attempted to validate the messages I was getting from Chang, especially the name he called her: "Butterfly." Whenever people from China came into our store, Francesca would talk to them about Chang.

She would also tell them that her name meant "butterfly." To her great disappointment, all of the Chinese-speaking people she spoke to would tell her that "Francesca" did not mean "butterfly" in Chinese. It did not even remotely sound like the word for butterfly. The word in Mandarin Chinese for butterfly is pronounced *hutier*. The more Francesca heard this, the more depressed she became.

"Why would my Baba give me wrong information?" Francesca said. "Everything else we have received has been right. Why would he get my name wrong? Perhaps I'm not the Butterfly Princess after all. Maybe all the messages have been wrong."

❀ Wrong Shipments

About a week went by, and then Francesca began to receive surprising affirmations that validated Chang's contention that her name truly was "Butterfly" in the seventeenth century. We did not pay that much attention to them at first, but it occurred so often that we eventually could not ignore them.

The first message came to her innocently enough. It was packed in a shipment from one of our store's giftware suppliers. In the midst of a large shipment of gift products from Chicago was a package of four golden butterfly pins. We checked with the company and found that this was not a mix up of product codes, or any other error in our order. These items were not supposed to be in the box at all. We were told to keep the pins as a gift.

Next, we received a shipment of posters from a supplier in Colorado. Among dozens of prints of angel-related scenes were two posters of a young Native American girl holding a bouquet of flowers, gazing transfixed at a swallowtail butterfly. The title of this print was "Little Butterfly" and it was captioned, "May you find a little joy in every ordinary moment."

We checked with this company, and found that these were sent by mistake. There was nothing in their records that showed these posters were sent to us. We were told to keep these posters as a gift, too.

Francesca was convinced that these accidental enclosures of butterflies in our merchandise shipments were messages from Chang. I was still skeptical, however. Then it happened again.

Our next delivery of gift items included a large box containing an expensive Austrian crystal figure of a golden butterfly. We again called the company. Our company representative, whom we had made the order with in person at a gift show in Los Angeles, assured us that she had not included this item on our order form.

"I have been your sales rep for the past nine years. I know you guys only purchase angel items. Why would I include a butterfly?" she said.

We had never had such a consistent string of wrong orders occur before. Receiving this many unordered golden butterflies was beyond my comprehension.

During this time, real butterflies began to visit us too. In particular, the swallowtail, a large golden butterfly with long tips on its wings. First, Francesca saw a swallowtail butterfly come to the entrance of our store, and then fly away. Next, when she was watering the garden in front of our house, a swallowtail came right up to her then flew over her head. Finally, when we stopped to put gas in our car, a swallowtail flew up to the car, stopped for a moment, and then fluttered away.

This many strange coincidences led Francesca and me to believe that we were receiving a message of some kind from the other side. Francesca suggested that I go into meditation and talk to Chang. She wanted me to find out what all these butterflies meant.

We waited until after we closed our store and went into our back room. There I began my meditation. After walking down my flight of ten stairs and following the path to the shimmering pond, I was able to find Chang.

"Chang, what's going on with all these butterflies, anyway?" I asked.

"I sent them for Francesca. How does she like them?" he asked.

"She loves them, but why are you sending them to her?" I asked.

"Gold is for light. Her name means 'butterfly,' and the swallowtail is her name," Chang replied.

I told Francesca about this message when I came back from my meditation. She said she was honored by Chang's gifts. She said she did not know that a spirit guide could send her gifts from heaven.

✾ More Proof

A few days later, a Chinese man visiting the United States on government business entered our store. We told him we had just visited Beijing, and how much we had loved it. Then Francesca remembered her butterfly. She went behind the counter and produced the poster of the Native American girl with a swallowtail butterfly.

Francesca showed the Chinese man the poster, pointed at the butterfly, and said "How do you say this in Chinese?"

The man looked at the poster and said, "*Hutier.*"

Undaunted, Francesca pointed at the butterfly again and said, "What kind of '*hutier*' is this?"

The man peered at the poster again for a few seconds and then replied. "Oh, we call this *hutier* a ,'*franchier*.'"

Francesca and I just stood and stared at each other for a moment.

"Well, it appears that you really are the Butterfly Princess, Francesca," I said, as I shook my head.

She looked back at me, and smiled. "I am your swallowtail butterfly."

CHAPTER EIGHT

Reincarnation

IN ORDER TO BETTER UNDERSTAND the relationship that Francesca and I have with Chang, and each other, it is important to know the concept of reincarnation and the history of this belief. Reincarnation is a belief that many people in our Western culture were not brought up with. Ironically, the majority of people on earth have faiths that include reincarnation in their doctrine. Furthermore, those faiths that do not include reincarnation in their doctrines today did embrace the concept of past lives at one time.

Totemism

The first known evidence of a belief in reincarnation goes back to ancient societies that existed 30,000 years ago. Cave paintings and artifacts suggest a belief system known today as "totemism." The word "totemism" comes from the Ojibwa "ototeman," which means "blood relationship." People with this belief system divided themselves into clans with human, animal, and plant totems. These totems were used in their creation myths and in the value systems of their tribes.

The Australian aborigine societies today practice a totemic religion that includes a belief in reincarnation from both human and animal incarnations. Theirs is the oldest practiced religion on earth. Many anthropologists theorize that all human religion was founded on the belief in reincarnation from humans and animals like those in contemporary totemistic cultures.

❀ Early Beliefs

The earliest written records on reincarnation are found in ancient Egypt. These go back to around 2000 BC. These records show how the human soul travels out of a person's body, but remains tied to their corpse. It was this belief that prompted the practice of embalming and mummification of the dead in Egypt.

The modern concepts of reincarnation go back to the Hindu texts of India from 1000 BC. These texts linked the reincarnation of the human soul to "karma." They felt that the soul passed from one plane to the other, carrying life impressions from past lives with it. These impressions were carried on in order to teach the soul new lessons needed to achieve full enlightenment. In Hinduism, one's liberation from the karmic cycle of life, death, and re-birth is the ultimate goal of earthly existence.

Tibetan Buddhism, founded around the year 1000, takes reincarnation to a different level. It blends the concepts of Buddhism, Hinduism, and Christianity. As in Hinduism, Tibetan Buddhists believe that we all go through a progression of incarnations on earth in order to increase karmic learning and ultimately break the karmic cycle of life and death.

They also believe that their religion's spiritual leadership is based upon the reincarnation of the spiritual and political aspects of the Buddha. The Dalai Lama, Tibet's spiritual and political leader, is acclaimed by many to be the reincarnation of both aspects of the Buddha. Followers of this faith believe that upon his death, the spirit of the Dalai Lama passes to a new body within nine months.

Like ancient Australian and Egyptian beliefs, Hinduism, and Tibetan Buddhism, Christianity and Judaism also have their roots in the belief of reincarnation. Many of the Hebrew tribes were named for animals, which appears to be a sort of totemism and thus shows an evolution from an original belief in reincarnation from humans and animals.

✸ Judaism

Judaism refers to reincarnation as *gilgul*. This Jewish belief has existed for thousands of years. This doctrine is believed in by Orthodox Jews, but was removed from the teachings of Eastern European Jews in the nineteenth century when a more modern "scientific" way of thinking became popular in Eastern European Jewish society.

In the Zohar, a book of great authority in Orthodox Judaism, this belief is stated very clearly:

All souls come in reincarnation and humans do not know the ways of the Lord and how the scales stand and how people are judged every day and time. How the souls are judged before entering this world and how they are judged after leaving it.

(Zohar, Mishpatim 32)

The Old Testament of the Christian Bible, originally taken from Hebrew Scriptures, also refers to reincarnation in the following verses:

Generations come and generations go, but the earth remains forever. The sun rises and the sun sets and hurries back to where it rises. The wind blows south and turns to the north; round and round it goes, ever returning on its course. All streams flow into the sea, yet the sea is never full. To the place where streams come from, there they return again. What has been will be again; there is nothing new under the sun. (Eccl 1:7-11)

❀ Christian Beliefs

Reincarnation beliefs in the Hebrew traditions continued into the time of Christ. Jewish tradition stated that the Messiah, foretold by their prophets, would not come to save the children of Israel until the prophet Elijah returned to earth in the flesh. When this is understood, the inclusion of John the Baptist in the New Testament of the Bible makes more sense.

In other words, before Christ could be acknowledged as the savior of the Children of Israel, John the Baptist had to be acknowledged as the reincarnation of the prophet Elijah. Christ himself made this known when he said:

> *For all prophets and the law has prescribed unto John. And if you receive it he is Elijah.* (Matthew 11:13-14)

Christ also acknowledged John the Baptist as Elijah when he said:

> *And he [John the Baptist] will go on before the Lord in the spirit of the power of Elijah.* (Luke 1:17)

Finally, and even more conclusively, Christ acknowledged the existence of reincarnation when speaking to his disciples about His coming to be their Messiah:

> *And the disciples asked him saying "Why then do the scribes say Elijah must come first" and he answered them saying "Elijah is indeed to come and will restore all things. But I say to you that Elijah has already come and they did not know him, but did to him whatever they wished. So also shall the Son of Man suffer at their hands."* (Matthew 17:10)

Reincarnation is not a radical concept in Christianity. For the first 300 years of the religion it was strongly believed in. As I have shown above, the story of Christ does not make sense, from a Jewish point of view, without reincarnation.

In an effort to maintain total power over the people of Rome, the Emperor Constantine had all references to reincarnation removed from the teachings of Christianity in the fourth century. In the sixth century, the Second Council of Constantine outlawed the teaching of reincarnation in the Christian faith. This belief has been forbidden in the teachings of the Christian church ever since.

❀ Dr. Brian Weiss's Findings

For the past seventeen centuries, most people of the Western world (there are currently over two billion Christians) have been under an illusion created by a religious system set up to control the masses. It tells them that they have only one chance to go to heaven, and only one lifetime to find their redemption.

It was not until 1988, when Dr. Brian Weiss revealed his eight-year research study on the existence of past lives that the Western prejudice against reincarnation began to change, with the publication of his book *Many Lives, Many Masters*. Dr. Weiss is a brilliant and very skeptical man who earned his Ph.D. in Psychiatry from Yale University in 1970. He had been a no-nonsense psychiatrist with little or no interest in anything spiritual, paranormal, or mystical. Dr. Weiss's life changed in 1980 when he began doing therapy on a woman he calls "Catherine."

Dr. Weiss describes Catherine as the most challenging patient that he ever encountered. She had numerous phobias, was prone to panic attacks, and had a hard time telling fantasy from reality. He tried numerous traditional forms of therapy for eighteen months, with no success. Finally, he decided to try hypnotherapy. He asked Catherine to go into a hypnotic trance and to go to the point in her life when her symptoms first arose. To Dr. Weiss's amazement, Catherine told him her psychosis began in the year 1863 BC, when she was a twenty-five-year-old woman named Amanda.

Dr. Weiss was shocked to find that Catherine could describe numerous lifetimes. Furthermore, he found that traumatic events and relationships from the past appeared to be the source of her current problems. After analyzing her for various psychiatric disorders and possible drug complications, Dr. Weiss began to accept Catherine's past life stories as true. Over a period of three years, he was able to end her phobias and panic attacks by having her recall events from her past lives.

During the past-life regression therapy sessions, Dr. Weiss was also surprised to receive messages from "Ascended Masters," also known as spirit guides, through Catherine. These entities gave him information about the nature of the universe, levels of consciousness, intuitive powers, and the nature of the soul. Dr. Weiss remained skeptical about the messages he was receiving until he was told about his father and the rare disease that took his life. He was also given a message about his three-week-old son who had died several years earlier. Dr. Weiss was especially amazed by these messages because they were about information that his patient Catherine had no access to.

Dr. Weiss's continuing study of past lives and the amazing results he has received have gained him much recognition in the scientific community. He led the study on the value of past-life regression in therapy at the University of Pennsylvania Medical School, and is a regular speaker at Yale University's Psychiatric Department. His work has led the federal government of the United States to fund projects studying the effects of past-life regression for the National Institute of Health's Office of Alternative Medicine.

Dr. Weiss believes that reincarnation has always been part of human consciousness. He feels that these beliefs have been revealed in the past, by psychics, dreams, déjà vu memories, and through meditation. His research shows that people live about one hundred lifetimes, not the thousands and thousands that some Buddhist sects speak of, before they choose to stay on the other side forever. Dr. Weiss's messages from the other side have told him that souls are immortal and have been around from the beginning of time.

CHAPTER NINE

Soul Groups

MANY EXPERTS ON REINCARNATION SPECULATE that souls migrate together from lifetime to lifetime. In this respect, many of the important people in your life, including your friends, parents, children, and even enemies, reincarnate together to work out karmic lessons from all of your past lives.

Soul mates are a good example of this. They are bonded souls who choose to unite as a couple from lifetime to lifetime; having shared many karmic experiences together, they choose to continue their relationship as they reincarnate as different people. Having this long-term karmic connection helps relationships grow and become more successful. Soul mates thus help each other reach their true potential much faster than first-time partners.

To test out my ideas about this, I decided to ask Chang who all the people we felt connected to in this lifetime were to him and us in the seventeenth century. To accomplish this task, I set up meditation sessions with many of the people we know, and then asked Chang if he knew them, and if so, who they were when they were with us in China.

❁ Brenda

Francesca and I met Brenda and her late husband Don ten years ago. They were our first major customers. A friend of theirs brought them to the store to see our gallery.

After Don died in 1996, Brenda became even closer to us. We took vacations to Las Vegas and even Rio De Janeiro together. We have always felt a connection with her and never knew quite what it was.

Shortly after our revelation of the identity of Chang, we went with Brenda and a group of our friends to walk a labyrinth at a local church.

When Brenda completed the path, she said, "I just saw Chang. He was holding my hand as I walked. He showed me a throne."

Francesca and I were amazed by Brenda's vision. I wondered how it could be. The next week, I did a meditation with her.

I asked, "Chang, was Brenda with us in seventeenth-century China?"

Chang smiled at me and nodded, "Yes."

I then inquired, "Who was she?"

"She was my third empress, Xioa Yi. Francesca and she were very good friends in our lifetime. I'm glad to see that they are still good friends now."

The next day I looked up the Kangxi Emperor on the internet. To my amazement, the name of his third empress was Xioa Yi. This was something I could never have made up, or even imagined.

❁ Kathryn D.

Kathryn, a tall and thin woman with short gray hair, in her late fifties, first met us as a customer during 1995. She has a Ph.D. in Psychology and runs a private clinical practice in Ventura. Although she is a trained scientist, she does believe in reincarnation and she wanted to know if she had any relation to Chang.

I did a meditation with Kathryn about a week after I met with Brenda.

"Chang, was Kathryn with us in the seventeenth century?" I asked.

"Yes, she was my fourth empress, Xioa Gong," he said.

I was amazed—another empress. I wondered about this name though. He was right with Brenda, but the chances of me getting two really strange Chinese names seemed next to impossible. The next day I looked up the names of Chang's empresses again. I was astounded to find out that the name of Kangxi's fourth empress really was Xioa Gong.

❀ Karen

In March of 2004, three women from Miami who had seen our Fox television program booked flights to California to see our store first-hand. They arrived around noon.

We gave these ladies the royal treatment. We showed them all the important things in our store. We took them to our shrine with thousands of prayers on it and then we took them to the gallery to see Andy Lakey's paintings. I played all the videos we had about the art, and they still wanted to know more about us. I told them what we knew at the time about Chang.

As I was telling these women about Chang, Karen, a tall woman with dark blue eyes, came into the gallery.

"Can I listen to your story?" she asked.

"Of course you can," I replied.

I continued to tell my stories and all listened intently. Karen and the three women from Florida spent several hours at our store before finally leaving for the day.

Three days later, Karen came back.

She walked up to Francesca and me, and said, "I need to talk to both of you about Chang."

"Oh, my God, you've seen him too," said Francesca.

"Yes," she replied. "I met him eight years ago. I was doing a job that not many women are successful at. I really wasn't trained to do it and didn't know what made me succeed. I asked God who's helping me anyway, and that was when I first saw Chang."

"What did he look like to you?" I asked.

"He looked just like you described him in the store," she said. "He was a tall, thin Asian man with a goatee and a long mustache. He was smiling at me through a window. When I saw him, I thanked him for his help."

Francesca was intrigued by Karen's story. "Keith, can you do a reading for Karen and find out if Chang knew her?"

"Sure," I said.

The store was empty, so I led Karen to the gallery in the back of the store and began to meditate. "Do you know Karen?" I asked.

"Yes, I do," Chang said as he nodded.

"Who was she?" I asked.

"She was someone I loved," replied Chang.

"Was she your lover?" I asked.

Chang gave me an angry look and said, "Don't you know that there are many kinds of love? Not all love is sexual. Karen was my sister."

Karen cried when I gave her this revelation. She still cries whenever we talk about Chang.

❀ Mary-Pat

We met Mary-Pat in the winter of 1996. She was a thirty-five-year-old woman with long curly strawberry-blond hair and deep blue eyes. Shortly after we met her, Mary-Pat's world fell apart. Her boyfriend of three years left her and she lost her night job as a waitress. She continued to work days for a very abusive boss at a local retail store.

In the summer of 1997, I hired Mary-Pat to work in our store while Francesca recovered from surgery. Mary-Pat quickly put our store's books in order and taught me how to run our store in a much more professional manner. In 1998 she met Howard, the love of her life, at our store. They had a whirlwind romance and shortly thereafter got married and she quit so she could help Howard run his business. They now have two beautiful children and live in an upscale neighborhood in Camarillo, California, located about ten miles from Ventura.

We have remained good friends with Mary-Pat through the years. One night in 2004, during a dinner at my home, she asked me, "Was I with you and Chang in the seventeenth century?"

"I saw you in a past-life regression," I told her.

"Who was I?" she asked.

"I don't know," I replied. "You looked like a Chinese man. I think you were sitting at a table eating noodles or something."

"Could you ask Chang who I was?" she asked.

I went into meditation and saw Chang.

"Who was Mary-Pat?" I asked.

"Don't you remember anything, Keith?" he said.

"No, I really don't know who she was," I replied.

"She was your brother," he said patiently. "He was my Minister of Finance at the palace. You had a very creative and influential family, Keith. I loved you all. I'm happy to see that you're all still together."

❀ Andy Lakey

I did not mean to meet Andy Lakey, or at least I did not think I did. Andy is the most famous living angel artist in the United States. His art is in the Vatican as well as the collections of numerous European royalty, Hollywood celebrities, and American presidents.

Andy claims that he learned to paint due to a meeting with angels in a near-death experience. He also had a spirit guide experience that led him to a mission of painting 2,000 angel paintings by the year 2000.

Andy has a very strong spiritual presence. His charismatic personality creates electricity in every room he enters. He has dark brown eyes, black hair, and sports a mustache.

Andy and his art were brought to my attention by a woman named Pam. She came to my store and insisted that I call him. She said she was a good friend of his, but turned out to be just a slight acquaintance. I made the call, and it resulted in my acquiring three pieces of Andy's art.

Ultimately, through taking orders at my store, I became his largest art dealer in the United States. We have been doing business together for ten years now and his art continues to sell very well in my store. We see each other regularly and talk every day by phone.

Andy Lakey's success as an artist has taken its toll on his health. During the late 1990s he signed a contract with a national art gallery network out of New York City. This organization demanded that he create over $70,000 worth of art each week. He rented a studio in Santa Barbara, California, and began working day and night to meet his art quotas. In the end, he developed a severe allergy to his paint that affected his immune system.

In the spring of 2004, Andy's wife Chantal called me. I told her how I had seen Andy in a past-life regression.

"He was Chinese in the seventeenth century," I said.

"What did he do there and how did that affect him in this lifetime? Why is he sick in this lifetime?" asked Chantal.

I went into meditation and saw Chang. "Who was Andy Lakey in the seventeenth century?" I asked.

"Keith," said Chang impatiently, "Andy was your half-brother. You came from a very influential family for one of Chinese origin. Your father had two wives. Andy was from wife number two. He owes you a karmic debt from that lifetime."

"What do you mean by that?" I asked.

"Didn't you ever wonder how your little store in the bad part of downtown Ventura could get such a famous artist to work with you? He remembers you, on some level of consciousness. His karmic debt has drawn him to you and made him sell his art at your store."

"What happened to Andy in the seventeenth century that led to his paint allergies in this lifetime?" I asked.

"I was very impressed by Andy's art and commissioned him to do some important artworks for my palace. He got sick and died and never finished his projects for me," said Chang.

"Andy is sick in this lifetime, too, but he did complete the 2000 angel paintings he was supposed to do in this lifetime," I said.

"Two other spirit guides and I gave Andy that assignment. I'm glad he could complete his mission this time. This is really good for him, karmically. Tell Chantal that he'll get better and will be able to paint again soon," said Chang.

I related this message to Chantal, and she was happy to know that Chang was with him as a spirit guide. She was also happy to know that Andy would soon resume painting.

❀ Laura

We met Laura on a rainy day in December of 1997. There had been a holiday street fair scheduled for downtown Ventura, but it had been canceled midway through due to the rain. A Latin-American woman in her early fifties with beautiful sparkling brown eyes ran into our store seeking refuge as the deluge of water fell from the sky. She was amazed to see the angel gift items and artworks that we sold. After this accidental meeting Laura became a steady customer and, in time, a very good friend.

Laura and her husband Jim became major collectors of Andy Lakey's art. We took them to his studio and to numerous art events. We eventually began to invite each other to dinner, as well as to both of our families' parties.

One day Laura came to our store and Francesca told her about our experiences with Chang. "Was I with you in the seventeenth century?" she asked.

"Keith can contact Chang and let you know," said Francesca.

I closed my eyes and went into meditation and soon met with Chang. "Was Laura with us in the seventeenth century," I asked.

"Yes, she was. Laura was my private guard." Chang showed me a suit of gray Chinese armor. It looked a little bulky and was not polished. It had scratches on it, too.

I told Laura what Chang told me, and what I saw in the meditation. She looked at me with amazement.

"I had a vision last week that I was wearing a suit of armor just like the one you just described," she said. Then she told me something I had not been aware of before. "The job I do at the Navy base where I work has to do with security. I always visualize myself in a suit of armor."

❀ Janet

We met Janet in 1999, when we began advertising with the local television station where she worked as an account executive. Janet now tells us that she did not believe in angels or spirit guides at the time, but her life and her beliefs have changed since she met us.

It was Janet who had introduced us to her friend Debbie in 2003, after I told her about Chang and she found that Debbie had the same spirit guide.

In 2004 Janet had a private session with me to answer some questions about her life and to see if she was with our soul group in the seventeenth century. I went into meditation and learned that Chang knew Janet.

"She was my astrologer. She showed me my lucky stars," he told me.

"Why did you need an astrologer?" I asked.

"An emperor needs to know what's going on all the time. He needs to know about the past, present, and the future to make the best decisions. Janet was my best astrologer. She gave me all the information I needed to make the best decisions to rule China."

❀ Debbie

We met Debbie in 2003 through Janet, and soon after, she began to teach the angel classes at our store.

One day, during a private session, Debbie requested: "Can you ask Chang who I was in the seventeenth century?"

"Why don't you ask him yourself? Isn't he your guide, too?" I asked.

"Keith, you can communicate with Chang much better than I do," she explained. "I've asked him questions like this and I just can't get a clear answer."

"Okay, let me try," I said.

I closed my eyes and counted down the ten steps to the path near a river where I always see Chang. He was standing there waiting for me.

"Hi, Chang," I said. "Debbie has asked me to find out from you who she was in the seventeenth century."

Chang smiled. "Tell Debbie that she was one of my ministers. She advised me about many things, including religion and astrology."

Debbie was happy to hear what Chang had told me. She then pointed to her throat and said, "I was born with this birthmark on my throat. It looks like a scar. Can you ask Chang if this has anything to do with my life in the seventeenth century?"

I went into meditation once more. When I asked him about the birthmark, he looked at me sadly and shook his head. "Debbie was beheaded at the end of her lifetime in China."

I told Debbie what Chang said. She looked a little concerned at first, but then smiled. "I always knew that my mark was a sign that I was executed in a past lifetime," she said.

❀ Rosie

Rosie first came to our store in 1996. She had learned that we sold art by Andy Lakey from a radio advertisement we ran, and wished to purchase a piece. She came with her friend Nina, who was a fundamentalist Christian. Rosie, a short Hispanic woman with long black hair, was very impressed by the art. Nina was concerned about whether it was really with God or not.

When Nina put her hand on one of the paintings, she had a vision of angels that convinced her and Rosie that our art, our store, and Francesca and I were on the right path. They have been good friends of ours ever since. They even helped us to move to our new house three years ago. Only true friends do that for you.

In the summer of 2004, Francesca and I visited Rosie and Nina at their home in Oxnard, California. After dinner, we spoke to them about Chang.

"Keith, do you think you could do a meditation here and talk to Chang for us?" asked Rosie.

"Sure, let me try," I replied. "Is there anything you'd like me to ask him for you?"

"Yes," said Rosie, "I would like to know if I was with him in the seventeenth century and if I so, who was I?"

Rosie's request caught me a little off guard. I was not sure how she felt about reincarnation.

When I asked Chang if he had known her, he told me: "Rosie was a priest. She worked at the palace as my astronomer. She helped me find a new calendar that worked better for China. I was the master of the calendar, and Rosie's assistance helped me gain more power and respect from my subjects."

"A new calendar? I wonder what that's all about," I thought to myself.

"Was Rosie Chinese?" I asked.

"No," Chang replied. "She was European. She was a Jesuit missionary."

✸ Nina

After I did the reading for Rosie, I was even more amazed when her friend Nina asked me to contact Chang and see if she was in the seventeenth century. Nina, a tall woman with long black hair, is of Philippine origin and knowing that she was a very devout Christian,

I was surprised that she would want to know anything about reincarnation.

When I asked Chang if he knew Nina, he showed me a clock. "She fixed my clocks," he said.

"You had clocks?" I said in surprise.

"Of course I did. I had lots of clocks," said Chang proudly. "Why wouldn't I have clocks?"

I told Nina the message. She looked at me shyly and softly said, "Keith, could you do me a big favor? Could you ask Chang what I should do with my life? I work as an electrician, and I love my work, but I can't get the good jobs because I'm not licensed."

I again contacted Chang and told him Nina's dilemma.

"Chang looked at me sternly, "Tell Nina that she has to get her license right away. She can't put this off anymore. It is really important."

I relayed this message to Nina and she seemed confused. "I don't have time to study for the license exam," she said. "I don't think I can pass it anyway."

"You should really listen to Chang," I said. "He's always right. If he thinks you can pass the test, I am sure you can pass it."

Six months after this reading, Nina took and passed her exam. She is now a licensed electrical contractor. And she thanks Chang for this accomplishment. She is certain that she could never have achieved it without his confidence and spiritual guidance.

❀ Peter Sterling

We have known Peter since 1996. He is a very charming and handsome man in his early forties. His charismatic magnetism and spiritual presence quickly endears him to everyone he meets.

Peter is a master harpist who performs with music groups throughout the world. His CDs are in high demand. They have won many music awards and are among the best selling in their genre. Peter also accompanies spiritual writers and artists on their speaking tours. He has played harp solos during the lectures of such people as Terry Lynn Taylor, Doreen Virtue, and Andy Lakey.

Peter says that his ability to play the harp was angelically inspired. He had never played the harp before he had a near-death experience in 1991. After that, the music poured out of him naturally. He has now made five award-winning CDs and is one of the most sought after harpists in the world.

In late 2004, Peter came to our store to see if we needed any more of his CDs. We purchased a dozen, and as he was about to leave, Francesca told him that we had just returned from China and explained that I was writing a book about my spirit guide.

"Oh, don't tell me he looks like Fu Manchu," said Peter astonished.

"How do you know that?" asked Francesca.

"I've seen him many times," said Peter. "I first saw him eighteen years ago."

You could have knocked Francesca down with a feather when she heard this. She was beside herself. She came to me and said, "Can you believe it, Keith? Chang is Peter's guide, too! Please go into meditation and find out for me who he was."

After we closed our store, I went into the art gallery and meditated. Chang came to me soon thereafter, and I asked him if Peter was there in the seventeenth century.

"Yes," said Chang. "He was my court musician. Like Andy Lakey, he didn't truly remember his talents in this life until he had a near-death experience. I'm happy to see that Peter is successful at his profession as a musician in this life."

✤ Katherine R.

Katherine R. first came to our store in 1995, and from the beginning we knew she was very spiritual. She put her hand on one of Andy's paintings and we saw angels come out of it. She did this several other times with a total of nine different people, and I was pretty much convinced that she could make things happen.

As I mentioned earlier in this book, it was Katherine who helped to convince me that Chang was real after we did a cable television program together in 2001. In 2004, we decided to find out just exactly who she was in relation to Chang and me in the seventeenth century.

Chang shook his head when I asked him who she was. "Keith, don't you remember her? She was your brother. Like you, she was very spiritual and she served as one of my religious ministers in the palace in the seventeenth century. I guided you to find her so that she could confirm my existence for you. It's because of Katherine that you now take me seriously. It's also her confirmation that convinced you to write your book about me."

❀ Richard

Francesca and I met Richard in 1995 when he visited our store for the first time with his wife Vicki. Richard is a short man of Jewish descent, with a scruffy black and gray beard. He dresses very casually, even for a tourist visiting Ventura.

We soon discovered that Richard was a criminal defense attorney from Pasadena, California (about an hour and a half away). Over the years, he and Vicki have become two of our dearest friends.

One evening, after we had gone to dinner together, Vicki asked me if I could go into meditation and ask Chang if she and Richard were with him in the seventeenth century. We went to their room at the Ventura Holiday Inn and there I did my meditation.

Chang confirmed that he did know Richard. "Richard was a Manchurian. I chose him to be in charge of the most important religious center in the country of China. I believe you call this the Temple of Heaven. This temple was important because our worship there assured good crops for the people of China. This was too important a task to give to someone of Chinese descent."

"How did Francesca and I know Richard in the seventeenth century?" I asked.

Chang shook his head and said, "Let me remind you, Keith. Richard was one of your fellow priests. You valued his counsel and he valued yours as well. My little butterfly would visit the Temple of Heaven and pray there. She was famous in those days and I am certain that Richard would go all out to impress her whenever she visited his temple."

✿ Vicki

After I had given Richard his message from Chang, Vicki was very anxious to hear what he had to say about her. Vicki is a Hispanic woman who has been confined to a wheelchair for the past five years. She helps manage her husband's law business and gives psychic classes and readings on the side. Vicki has a degree in psychology and is an ordained minister. She has also studied under some of the most famous psychics in the United States.

I went back into meditation and again saw Chang, who was still standing where I had left him moments before. "Did you know Vicki in the seventeenth century?" I asked.

"Yes, I did," said Chang.

He then showed me piles of coins. "She counted the money in China," he said.

"Was she some sort of tax collector?" I asked.

"Yes, she collected the money. I would send her all over China to collect the money," said Chang.

I told Vicki what Chang had told me, and was surprised by her response.

"This makes sense to me," she said. "I was always a great math student in school. I was at the top of my classes in algebra, geometry, and calculus. I use my talents in math every day to run our law practice."

"I didn't know that you were so into math," I said.

"How did I know you guys in the seventeenth century?" she asked.

I went back into meditation, and Chang explained that I had not known Vicki very well. "Francesca knew her when she was my little butterfly," he said. "Vicki was her math teacher. I believed in providing education to all my children, both my boys and my girls. Later in her life, Vicki brought my little butterfly messages from me and my little butterfly would give messages to her to bring back to me."

"What does that mean?" I asked.

"It means that Vicki was a tax collector and she was also my messenger," said Chang.

❀ Renfield

In 1989, I was recruited from a fundraising job in San Jose, California, located about five hours north of Ventura, to join a religious organization for troubled young people out of state. Frank, the organization's president, flew to California to meet me and we formed a warm and lasting friendship.

In the end, I accepted the position and moved to Kansas. The lifestyle change was like culture shock for my family and me. We went from owning a small townhouse on the east side of San Jose to purchasing a four-acre country estate. This was the best of times for us, but it was about to become the worst of times.

Soon after accepting my new position, I learned that Frank had hand-picked a man called Renfield as his successor. This was not a major concern for me at the time, because Frank did not plan to retire for at least five more years.

As I became more accustomed to the working environment of the organization, I began to hear negative things about Renfield. I soon learned that although he gave a first impression of being kind, gentle, and loving, that this was just a facade. In reality, he was negative, vindictive, and abusive to everyone. I brought this message to Frank. He realized that he had been duped by Renfield and had made a big mistake.

Frank tried to get this information to our board of directors, but it was too late. Renfield had already charmed them with his facade of loving kindness. In the end, it was Frank who lost his job, as the board of directors offered him a mandatory early retirement.

I was now stuck with the impossible job of trying to please Renfield. He told me the first day he took over as president that he did not like me, and that he felt that a priest should have been in my position. I had twenty years of successful experience in my field. I was indignant.

As the next year passed, my relationship with Renfield got even worse. I doubled the organization's funding and significantly increased their image and name recognition throughout the United States. Still, Renfield gave me a bad evaluation report.

Ultimately, Renfield fired me on what I knew were false grounds of incompetence. I knew his real motive. He wanted to replace me with a priest.

We left with great sadness and humiliation. We lost our beautiful country estate, we lost our car, and in the end we lost our dignity. We ended up living with my parents in Oxnard, California. I could not find work, so I put in for public assistance. It took me three years to get my life back together and open our store in 1995.

One night, during our meditation class in 2004, I did a past-life regression. During this regression I returned to my life in China. There I met Renfield. I was amazed and appalled to find that he was one of Chang's sons and I knew him then. Even worse, I learned of how I had died in that lifetime. As Chang's son, Renfield had ordered my execution. My head and hands were chopped off. It was an awful and very humiliating way to be killed.

Looking back at what happened to me with Renfield in this lifetime, I can see that it was really a karmic experience. Unbeknown to Renfield and to me at the time, he had done me a great favor by firing me. If I had stayed at my position, I would have continued to live a lazy, laid-back lifestyle in my beautiful estate and I would have never fulfilled my life's destiny. Thanks to Renfield, I am now completing my life path through writing my fourth spiritual book. I have also been ordained as a minister in the Church of Religious Science. My suffering was ultimately rewarded, my books and my ministry have helped thousands of people throughout the world to live fuller, happier lives.

❀ Thanking Chang

One night, after we had done readings for several of our friends, Francesca decided to say a few words. "Thank you, Baba, for bringing us together with such wonderful friends," she said.

I meditated and communicated Francesca's message to Chang.

"It's very nice that Francesca feels that way about her friends," said Chang. "I can't take credit for this. I really didn't bring you together. Souls flock together like gazelles. They do this for karmic reasons. In this lifetime you've come from all over the world to accomplish one mission. The mission all of you share is one of peace. I know it's going to take more than seventeen people to make this happen. It will probably take more than seventeen million people to accomplish this goal, but you and your soul group are the beginning of this process."

CHAPTER TEN

Chang in History

ONCE I REALIZED THAT CHANG was actually the seventeenth-century Kangxi Emperor of China, I began to do extensive library and internet research about him. I had studied the history of the Western world while in college, but I soon realized that I was totally ignorant of Chinese history. This is a subject that is rarely covered by Western education systems and I had never bothered to study it on my own.

I found that to truly understand the significance of Chang, I first had to realize that Asia has more history and has been more impor-tant in forming Western lifestyles than any other part of the world. China, in fact, is the oldest civilization on earth.

China left behind the Neolithic era of hunters and gatherers to become a kingdom around 2100 BC. At that time the first Chinese dynasty, the Xia (Chia), was founded. Since that time there have been 308 emperors and eighteen dynasties in this ancient land.

This civilization and many that followed over the next 4,000 years were the most advanced on earth for their time. The Chinese invented numerous things that we now take for granted, including paper and paper currency; gun powder and fireworks; iron casting; printing and the first printed book; the magnetic compass; the kite; and even pasta.

The modern country of China was significantly influenced by the last three dynasties, the Yuan, the Ming, and the Qing. It was these three dynasties that molded the country we today know as China.

❀ The Yuan Dynasty

The Chin Dynasty of China was conquered by Mongolian armies led by Genghis Khan in 1215. Following Genghis Khan's death in 1227, his grandson Kublai Khan succeeded him and established the Yuan Dynasty.

Under the rule of Kublai Khan, China became the largest land-based empire in the history of the world. It stretched from Korea and Western Russia in the north to Burma and Iraq in the south. Kublai Khan and the Mongolians had no experience in government administration, so they adopted Chinese political models.

Although the Mongolian leaders of China adopted the role of Chinese emperor, they failed to unite the Chinese people behind them. One of their greatest mistakes was setting up a class system made up of four castes. These were:

1. The Mongolians
2. Non-Chinese people from inner Asia
3. The people of Northern China (the Han)
4. And lastly, the people of Southern China (The Nar)

The Mongolians enjoyed the greatest privileges, while the Nar had the least. These privileges applied to taxes and the penal code. Mixed marriages were prohibited and it was impossible to gain promotion from one caste to another.

During the 1340s and 1350s, the Mongolian empire began to break down. Corruption, political rivalries, and a succession of natural disasters all led to its downfall. A peasant rebellion followed, defeating the Mongolian troops and forcing the last Yuan emperor and his court to flee China. The Mongolians were so weakened by this episode that it was not until the fifteenth century that they regained sufficient strength to extend their empire's borders once again.

✿ The Ming Dynasty

In 1368, rebel leader Zhu Yuanzhang, historically known as Emperor Taizu, became the first emperor of the Ming Dynasty. The Yuan Dynasty had lasted ninety-six years with eleven emperors. It was the Yuan that moved the political, economic, and cultural center of China to Beijing.

The Ming Dynasty was the last native Chinese dynasty to rule the empire. The Ming reunited the area now known as China under Chinese rule. The dynasty reached its height of power in the fifteenth century. At this point they controlled all of Mongolia and Tibet. This was a very prosperous period for China as their population soared to over 100 million people. The Chinese believed themselves to be the most advanced civilization on earth.

The Ming Dynasty was also known for its strong and complex central government, which unified and controlled the population. Ironically it was this complexity that also prevented the Ming government from adapting to changes in society and eventually led to its downfall.

By the last years of the Ming Dynasty, the economy of China was faltering. Long wars, numerous hostile attacks by Japan, and a peasant uprising in 1627 made the Ming's financial situation even worse. Furthermore, Chinese peasants were unable to meet the ever-increasing tax burden and abandoned their fields. This led to an economic crisis for the dynasty.

In 1644, troops led by rebel leader Li Zicheng captured Beijing. On seeing the approaching army, Emperor Chongzhen committed suicide. Li Zicheng negotiated the terms of surrender with the Ming army commander, Wu Sangul.

Rather than accept Zicheng's terms, Wu Sangul made an alliance with the invading Manchurian army leader, Prince Dorgon, to fight the rebel troops. Dorgon and his troops defeated the rebels, but then invaded and eventually took control of China from the Ming Dynasty.

The Ming Dynasty lasted 276 years with sixteen emperors. The new Manchurian Empire, known as the Qing Dynasty, would be the last Chinese government ruled by emperors. It was during this period that imperial rule reached its highest level of power and influence.

✸ The Qing Dynasty

The Manchurians that formed the new Qing Dynasty were originally pastoral nomads who established a powerful military force. They captured Korea and parts of Mongolia, and when given the opportunity, captured China. They felt they were an ethnically elite group, and forbid intermarriage with the native Chinese.

Emperor Shunzhi of Manchuria was the first emperor of the Qing Dynasty to rule China. In 1643, at the age of five, he became emperor upon the death of his father Hong Taiji. Actual power lay in the hands of his regents, Princes Dorgon and Jirglang. In 1644, the Qing Dynasty was proclaimed as the legal successor of the Ming Dynasty.

Shunzhi's mother was Empress Dowager Xia-Chuang, who was an excellent politician. She helped the young emperor maintain his power and learn to rule. In 1650, when Shunzhi was only twelve years old, Prince Dorgon died and Shunzhi took over the leadership of China.

During his short reign as emperor, Shunzhi encouraged the Chinese nationals to participate in government. He also hired them to teach his children. Shunzhi had three sons. In 1661, a smallpox epidemic hit China. Shunzhi and his family were struck by this illness. Shunzhi's favorite concubines and two of his sons died. Four months afterward, Shunzhi contracted the disease and died, leaving his only living son Xuanye as the heir to the throne, at age seven. He was made the Kangxi Emperor of China on February 17, 1661, only twelve days after his father's death.

The Kangxi Emperor preferred to be called by the title Chang (meaning "Son of Heaven"). This title reflected his position as father of the Han nation and guardian of its traditions. It also reflected his position as the emperor of China and continued a trend begun during the Ming Dynasty where emperors were granted the title Chang after their deaths.

Chang was the son of a concubine named Zhuang. She was the daughter of a Mongolian prince of the Borjidid Clan. Her ancestry traced back to the Yuan Dynasty leaders Kublai Khan and Genghis Khan.

Zhuang was officially given the status of Manchurian when she was made an empress by Shunzhi. Empress Xiao Kang died in 1663, leaving Xuanye an orphan at age nine. His grandmother, Empress Dowager Xia-Chuang (whose name was Bochita), raised him from this point on.

Chang was considered a much more compassionate and tolerant leader than the emperors of the Ming period. He was best known for being frugal, practical, and conscientious in his governing of China. Chang was said to be tall, well built, and in possession of a lively mind. He had an excellent memory, good judgment, a marked taste for study, and a steady temperament, coupled with a great self image. During his reign, China increased in wealth and most of the time enjoyed peace and prosperity.

Domestically, Chang established several large-scale public works projects. These included repairing the "Grand Canal" to transport rice to feed the northern population of China, and dredging and banking the Huang He (Yellow River) to prevent flooding. He also greatly reduced taxes and opened four ports to foreign ships to increase trade with the West.

During this period, China became the largest country on earth. Through war and alliances, Chang annexed Tibet, Taiwan, Outer Mongolia, and parts of Russia into his kingdom.

Chang's rule was noted for its advancements in learning. In order to bring Chinese scholars into the Qing fold, he summoned them to compete in a special examination. He selected the best of the scholars and calligraphers to be his personal secretaries. Chang's project led to the creation of numerous esteemed works of art and literature for

China, including the Kangxi Dictionary and the history of the Ming Dynasty.

More than anything else, Chang was interested in the field of Western science. In 1668, he became involved in a controversy concerning Chinese and Western calendar methods. To his great concern he found that the Jesuit priests sent by the Roman Catholic Church were more knowledgeable about the exact measurement of the year than his high officials. He placed the Jesuit missionaries in charge of the Imperial Board of Astronomy. He also had them teach him the art of Western Science. In the last years of his rule, Chang even arranged to have a group of Chinese and Manchurian scholars be tutored by the Jesuits.

In the beginning of Chang's reign, Catholic missionaries were often persecuted. In 1692, he issued a decree called the "Edict of Tolerance," which legalized and protected missionary work in the empire. This edict permitted the practice of Christianity on the condition that converts continued to perform ancestral rites. The Jesuits considered these rites not as worship but a civic rite of commemoration of lost loved ones.

In 1693, after the Jesuit priests cured Chang of malaria with quinine, he gave the priests a piece of land inside of the Imperial Palace to build a church on. The Jesuits also founded communities in south and central China.

To the Dominican and Franciscan missionaries, however, the rites allowed to the Chinese by the Jesuits looked like superstition. They made reports to Pope Clement XI telling of the heresy allowed by the Jesuits.

In 1704, the Sacred Congregation for the Propagation of the Faith (The Inquisition) prohibited the policy of Catholic priests accepting the practices of Chinese ancestor worship or Confucianism.

In 1705, Pope Clement XI sent a delegation to China to find out what his missionaries were doing. He was especially concerned about the Jesuit's acceptance of Chinese belief systems, which the Vatican considered a heresy.

Chang was infuriated by this action from the Vatican. He considered this to be interference with Chinese matters. He summoned the delegation's leader to an Imperial audience in 1706. This meeting was disastrous and showed that the Vatican had no understanding of Chinese beliefs (especially Confucianism) yet still condemned them. This led to the end of Christianity in China.

Chang had four empresses and thirty concubines. He had thirty-six sons (twenty reached adulthood) and twenty daughters (eight reached adulthood). Chang ruled longer than any emperor in Chinese history. His accomplishments as an emperor set the standard for the entire Qing rule. The Qing Dynasty lasted 268 years. There were ten emperors during this time. Chang laid the foundation for the longest period of peace, prosperity, and political stability in China's history, and is today considered China's greatest leader.

CHAPTER ELEVEN

Our Return to Beijing

BY JUNE OF 2004, FRANCESCA and I felt we had come a long way on our journey to find the meaning of messages my spirit guide Chang was giving us. We had learned his role in our lives and we had learned who he was in Chinese history. We had also learned the role he had played in our karmic destiny. There was still, however, much more for us to learn. We felt that the only way to achieve this knowledge was to return to Beijing.

This time I decided that I did not want to be constricted by a tour group, so I booked our flights and rooms myself for October of 2004. We decided we would get around using local transportation and tourist resources. We would use guide books and our past knowledge to see points of interest.

Our friend Brenda, whom Chang had identified as one of his empresses, was so intrigued by our adventure that she asked to come with us. I booked her a flight and accommodations too. I felt that Brenda's recent enlightenment about Chang and her newly found connection to China might be part of the karmic lesson that Francesca and I were destined to learn.

✿ A Class in Mandarin Chinese

In July of 2004, I found to my great excitement that Ventura Community College was offering a six-week course titled "Beginning Mandarin Chinese." Francesca, Brenda, and I each paid our $70.00 course fees and signed up.

We found that Mandarin Chinese is one of the most widely spoken languages on earth. Over 95 percent of the people in China speak this dialect. We wanted to get started learning this language right away. We spent much time together discussing how we were going to make our way through China on our own and surprise everyone we met there with our amazing linguistic abilities.

As we got further into our studies of the language, we found something very discouraging and really quite scary. Mandarin Chinese is perhaps one of the most difficult languages to learn. It is a tonal language with four separate and phonemically distinct tones. This means that even if you say the right words in Chinese, if your tone is just a little off, the difference in meaning could be as great as the difference between calling someone your mother or calling them your horse.

We were further discouraged to find that people in our class who had lived in China for several years still could not communicate in Mandarin well enough for our instructor to understand them.

Francesca, Brenda, and I became more concerned with each class we took. By the time the course was over in early September, we were convinced that we would probably never be able to speak or understand a language which had been our native tongue just over 300 years before in our past lives.

We knew that on our trip we would have to use the little Chinese we had learned, along with a lot of creative tourist tricks, in order to survive. We were taking no organized tours and we had no personal contacts with anyone in China. We were really going to be on our own this time.

✿ A Wild Ride in Beijing

We left LAX on Tuesday, October 13, 2004. The flight seemed very long, but was smooth and uneventful. It looked as though I had put together the perfect trip to China.

We landed at the Beijing International Airport right on time, and by 5:00 PM, we had recovered our luggage and were ready to catch a taxi to our hotel. This was not as easy a task as one might think.

The luggage pickup area is on one side of the airport, while the taxi station is at the far end about half a mile away. When you have been traveling for about twenty-four hours, this appears to be a very difficult distance to negotiate.

The airport was full of young men offering taxi rides to town. It is about a half hour trip to Beijing by cab, so getting a ride is essential. All of the tour-guide books warn you of the unauthorized taxi services out of the Beijing airport. These unethical people prey on unsuspecting tourists and gouge them with high fares and low quality cabs. I did not want this to happen to us, but it did.

A young Chinese man, who appeared to be in his early twenties, approached us about a cab ride to our hotel in Beijing. I was very suspicious about his proposition.

"Does your cab have a meter?" I asked.

"Meter yea!" he replied in broken English. "Taxi have meter. Yea, yea, no worry, is real taxi."

We followed the man across a wide roadway to a large parking structure, pulling our large suitcases behind us. As we walked across the street, I noticed, to my concern, that there was a line of taxis far to the right of us.

"Isn't that where we should be going?" I asked.

The Chinese man motioned us to hurry up and pointed forward. "Your cab in here," he said pointing to the parking structure.

We were all too exhausted to protest. We followed him like zombies.

We entered the parking structure and the man motioned for us to follow him up the elevator. We went to the top level. Most of the lights at this level of the parking structure were out. Everything was dark and foreboding.

We walked across the parking lot to where two of the man's accomplices were waiting. Each grabbed one of our bags and began to run with it. We chased them at our best pace considering our state of exhaustion.

We watched as the men rounded a bend, at which point I began to think they were trying to steal our bags. We all ran to catch up with them. Francesca kept up pretty well, but Brenda was falling behind, so I tried to stay near her. Then I heard a loud thump behind me. Brenda had tripped and fallen over a pipe that lay on the concrete floor. She was moaning. At first I thought she might have broken a bone, and that our trip was over before it had begun.

I helped Brenda up. She seemed bruised, but all right other than that. I had her put her arm over my shoulder as I led her onward.

"I know that you're hurt, but we have to catch up with those men. I'm afraid for Francesca's safety," I said.

We staggered around the bend and found Francesca and the two men standing in front of a battered red taxi. I was relieved to see that Francesca was fine, and that we had not been robbed.

I walked over to the driver of the cab and asked, "Do you know how to get to the Courtyard by Marriott Hotel?"

He looked at me blankly. I showed him a slip of paper I had with the name and address of my hotel written in Chinese. He studied this for a moment and shook his head, indicating "Yes."

"How much will it be to drive us to our hotel?" I asked.

"Two hundred yuan" (a little over $20.00), the man replied.

I did not know if this was a good price or not, but I was too tired to argue, Brenda was injured, and I knew we would never find our way back to catch another cab at the airport. I accepted the man's price for our trip to town.

We put our baggage into the cab and got in. Due to her injuries, we decided to let Brenda sit in the front seat. Francesca and I sat in the rear of the cab. The taxi was in terrible condition and looked like it had been scrapped from service many years earlier. It did have a meter, but it was broken. There were no seat belts or passenger restraints of any kind. We were at the mercy of our driver.

He tore out of the airport parking lot like a banshee out of hell, cutting off two other cabs and shouting what sounded like obscenities at them as he went by. Screeching onto the freeway, he cut off another driver and moved into the fast lane. Then he cut over two lanes to the right without signaling and cut off another car, all the time honking his horn like a madman. We all knew, then, that we had made a major mistake in taking this cab.

For Brenda, being in the front of the cab gave her an even more terrifying view of the action. This would have been bad under any circumstances, but with her recent injuries, the jostling back and forth by our road-raged driver brought her both more pain and fear.

When we finally arrived in the city of Beijing, we thought our troubles were almost over, but we were wrong. To my great concern, I noticed that our driver was going in circles as though he was lost. His seeming lack of direction appeared to bring on even more reckless tendencies in his behavior. He cut off four more cars and a city bus and pulled to a stop in front of a large hotel with a red neon sign on top of it. Then he motioned for us to get out.

Looking closely at the hotel, my heart sank. This was not the Courtyard by Marriott. It was some other Chinese tourist hotel.

I took the paper from my pocket and pointed to it. "This is not our hotel!" I shouted.

The driver argued with me in Chinese, and again gestured for us to get out of his cab. Considering the insane driving style of this driver, I thought about getting out and trying to find another cab. But we were off the beaten path, exhausted, and Brenda was hurt. I knew we had to stay the course.

The driver took the paper with the hotel information on it from my hand and made a call on his cell phone. He talked for a moment and then said, "Fifty yuan (about $5.00) more to take you to hotel."

I was furious. "You're a thief and this is robbery!" I shouted.

The driver screamed back at me in Chinese. Then he opened the doors of his cab and threatened to throw us all out in the middle of nowhere. I knew we were stuck. I screamed a few choice American cuss words at the driver and finally agreed to pay him the additional fifty yuan.

The driver screeched off again, even more road-raged than before. To our great concern, he still did not look like he knew where he was going. He cut people off left and right. He went to corners and made wild "U" turns. Things seemed hopeless. We wondered if we would ever reach our hotel.

In the midst of this chaos, Francesca had an idea. "Keith. Brenda. We've got to pray," she said. "This driver's crazy, and I don't think he's ever going to get us to our hotel. Baba brought us here to Beijing, and we've got to ask for his help now. We all have to pray. We all have to make contact with Baba."

I did not know if this was the best idea in the world, but considering the circumstances, I felt anything was worth a try. "Chang, please help us!" we all said in unison. "Chang, please help us find our hotel!"

Just then there was a loud "BANG" from the right side of the cab. At first I thought it was a firecracker, or possibly a gunshot. The driver appeared startled, but kept driving in his insane style.

At the next stoplight, another cab driver pulled up next to us and made a pointing gesture with his hand toward the right side of the cab. Our driver began to scream more obscenities. I knew right away that we had blown a tire.

The driver pulled off to a median in the center of a very busy street, and then motioned for us to get out of the cab. He opened his trunk for us to retrieve our suitcases, then got on his cell phone and screamed, more upset than ever, to someone on the other end of the line.

As we pulled our suitcases out of the trunk, another taxi pulled up and offered to take us to our hotel. I showed him the piece of paper with the address in Chinese. He seemed to know where it was. I handed our road-raged driver a two hundred yuan bill and packed our bags in the trunk of the new taxi. The new driver took us to our hotel in less than five minutes. He drove tranquilly and safely. The cost for this ride was only twenty yuan (about $2.00).

It was about 7:00 PM when we finally arrived at the Courtyard by Marriott. The service was efficient and courteous. We were given a room on the twenty-fourth floor of the massive hotel. The rooms were even more beautiful than we had expected—overlooking a busy market district with the ever-emerging Beijing skyline, lined with numerous cranes and construction equipment, off in the distance. Francesca and I climbed into our bed and in our exhausted state immediately fell fast asleep.

The next morning we awoke early. We could see the bustling business activities of modern Beijing taking place far below us. It was truly exciting to be in China again.

Francesca told me that she had experienced a dream while we slept the night before. In the dream, an elderly Native American couple, a man and a woman, had visited her. The couple told Francesca that we were under their protection. They particularly stressed that they were protecting us from "witchcraft." They told Francesca that if she wanted to talk with them more, she could visit them anytime she wanted. The man drew Francesca a map that showed her where to find them. Francesca was concerned because she awoke and did not remember what was on the map. Francesca, Brenda, and I had set an aggressive agenda for our trip. We felt it would be most appropriate to start with a visit to the Imperial Palace. We were happy to find that Brenda had not suffered any major effects from her fall the evening before. All she had to show for the incident was a heart shaped bruise on her knee. The three of us went to breakfast together and discussed our evening's adventure and our plans for the day.

The breakfast, which was included in the price of the room, was excellent. It consisted of an elegant buffet that featured both Western and Chinese specialties. We all ate heartily and were so stuffed that we went back to our rooms to relax before taking our outing to the Imperial Palace.

When Francesca and I returned to our room, Francesca asked if I would meditate and talk to Chang for her. She said she had some questions she would like for him to answer.

I was curious.

"I'd like to know the meaning of my dream last night," she explained. "Who were the Native American couple I saw and what did they mean by 'witchcraft'?"

I agreed to do the meditation for her. I calmed my mind, and took deep breaths. I counted my descent down ten steps to a path, and then walked to a lake by a waterfall where I saw Chang standing, waiting for me.

"Keith!" he said, "It's nice to have you back in China. How did you like the Native Americans I sent you?"

"Who were those Native Americans?" I asked. "Francesca saw them in a dream last night."

"Those are your protector guides for this trip," said Chang. "I thought you might need extra help, so I sent two. Didn't they help you last night?"

"What do you mean by that?" I said. "I didn't see that we got much help at all last night. We were nearly robbed, killed, and abandoned."

"Keith, it was your free will to pick the taxi you took. It was the spirit guides that I sent you that finally took action and shot arrows at the tire of that maniac driver who was trying to rob you, so you could escape," said Chang.

I asked Chang about the guides' reference to "witchcraft."

"Oh, those Native American guides are always talking about 'witchcraft,'" said Chang. "To them, anything that has to do with modern technology is 'witchcraft.' They saw you were in trouble with that 'bewitched' taxi and took action by shooting their spiritual arrows at it. It worked, didn't it?"

"Yes," I agreed. "Thank them for their help," I added.

❀ Back to the Imperial Palace

On Thursday, October 15, Francesca, Brenda, and I decided to go on our first outing. The Imperial Palace was only about two miles from our hotel.

I went to the hotel concierge and asked him to write our destination in Chinese so that we could give it to our taxi driver. I also obtained the name and location of our hotel, so that we could get back. We went outside and asked one of the hotel attendants to hail a cab for us. When Francesca and I first visited the Imperial Palace, our tour had taken us to Tiananmen Square and we had entered through the Meridian Gate. We quickly realized that our driver was not taking us to Tiananmen Square, but out toward the other end of town. We were at the Gate of Divine Prowess, the rear entrance to the palace.

Francesca and I were a little disorientated at first. Now we had to take our tour backwards. We climbed up and down massive stairways to the various halls in the palace.

"Keith, can we go somewhere in this place where there aren't so many stairs?" asked Brenda.

"Let me see what I can do," I replied. "The last time we visited the palace our tour guide herded us through like cattle. We missed a lot. There are many places we can go here that don't have stairs. Let's get out of the main area and see what we can find."

We walked to the far side of the complex and found the "Nine Dragon Screen." This much-prized mosaic was created in 1773 of shiny ceramic tiles. It is ninety-six feet long, and nearly twelve feet wide. The dragon is the symbol of Imperial rule, and this mosaic is considered the best rendering of that symbol.

Across from the wall, in a former residence for a prince, was something I had wanted to see: The Clock Museum. This is located in the Hall of Worshiping Ancestors. We paid an additional admission charge, and entered the facility. The Clock Museum was amazing. It had the best collection of extravagant timepieces I had ever seen. This included everything from intricate mechanical clocks to solid gold clocks encrusted with jewels. Most of these clocks were from the seventeenth and eighteenth centuries, made in France and England.

This museum was especially important to us, because Chang had told us that our friend Nina had been in charge of fixing clocks at the palace during his reign as emperor. We wanted to take some photos of these clocks to show Nina when we returned home.

We spent about an hour in this museum, and then we walked out of a passageway to a beautiful courtyard called the "Qianlong Garden." At the far end of this courtyard was the "Gate of Heavenly Purity." At the other side of this gate was the "Palace of Heavenly Purity," which was where Chang had lived.

Here, we found a former princess residence that had been made into a gift shop and photo opportunity spot for Chinese tourists. For a small fee, one could don the costume of an emperor, empress, or princess, and have one's photo taken in the royal bedchamber. This was something very appealing to the Chinese, since up until the fall of the Qing Dynasty in 1911, a commoner would have been beheaded if they were caught dressing like royalty.

Brenda and I tried to convince Francesca to put on the garb of a royal princess. At first she resisted. She felt it would be too much trouble to change her clothes in a courtyard of the Imperial Palace. After more pleading, we finally convinced Francesca. She ran over to the woman running the concession and motioned that she wanted to put on the princess costume.

I paid the woman the money to rent the costume, and Francesca put it on. To our surprise she was immediately transformed into the Butterfly Princess. It was amazing—Francesca is Nicaraguan, but in this costume the Chinese workers and tourists at the Imperial Palace all asked her if she was Chinese.

Francesca smiled and answered, "I'm not Chinese. I'm Manchurian."

Brenda and I took several photos of Francesca in her princess costume. I later put one of them on my computer as my background wallpaper. Many of the people who see this display ask me who the person in this photo is. Very few people realize that the Qing Princess in the photo is really Francesca.

Francesca, Brenda, and I spent over four hours exploring the Imperial Palace. We all felt that we had been able to take our time and really experience the palace the way it should be visited. We exited through the Meridian Gate at Tiananmen Square, where we walked around for about half an hour. Unlike our experience during our previous visit, this time we were not mobbed by aggressive street vendors. We just enjoyed the warm October's day as we viewed the communist monuments around the area. From there we crossed the street to a commercial district, and found a restaurant where the three of us ate lunch, before taking a cab back to our hotel.

I later found out something very interesting about our trip that morning to the Imperial Palace. The rear entrance to which our driver had taken us, the Gate of Divine Prowess, was not the official entrance used by the emperor and visiting government officials and international dignitaries. This was, instead, the gate used by people employed by the emperor, such as advisors, accountants, and teachers, who lived in the nearby residences known as *hutongs*. This was also the entrance used by the members of royal family and the emperor's concubines. This would have been the entrance that we had all used when we were last together in the palace in the seventeenth century.

It did seem strange at the time, after the very explicit instructions by our hotel staff, that our cab driver would take us to the wrong place. I really do not believe in coincidences anymore. I feel that we were brought to the Gate of Divine Prowess for a reason. Somehow, it appears that our cab driver was guided. Maybe he knew us from a past life, or perhaps he received a message from Chang that made him divert us to that spot. We were brought there to learn who we were, and how we entered and exited the Imperial Palace during our past life.

❁ A Multi-Colored Butterfly

That night I meditated again and met with Chang. He told me that Francesca was his little butterfly, and that she looked beautiful as a princess. He added that it was really good to see her dressed as a princess again after all these years.

Francesca also asked Chang about her aunt Rosa Adilia, who had died of lung cancer two days before we left for Beijing. Her aunt's funeral was the next day, and Francesca was very sad that she was going to miss it.

"Baba, where is my Tiita?" (Tiita translates to "little aunt" in Spanish, and was the name she always referred to her aunt by) asked Francesca. "Is she in heaven with you?"

"Don't worry about your aunt," said Chang. "She was a sad butterfly with you on earth, but she is a happy butterfly in heaven. When you get home, ask your family about the butterfly at her funeral. They'll know what I'm talking about." We later found out that a butterfly had followed all of Francesca's family members throughout the entire service in the cemetery in Los Angeles.

"Will I also receive a sign from my aunt tomorrow?" asked Francesca.

"You will receive a sign tomorrow, when you go to the Summer Palace. This sign will show you that your aunt is with you. You will see a beautiful butterfly. It will be like no butterfly you've ever seen before. It will be many different colors."

"Baba, did you know my aunt?" asked Francesca.

"Yes," said Chang, "your aunt was with us in the seventeenth century. I knew her and you knew her too. Your aunt chose to pass when she did so that she could take this trip with you. You'll believe me when you see the sign she brings you tomorrow."

❀ The Night Market

That night we decided to go to what they call the "Night Market." This was one of the places that we had missed during our last trip. This market was established in 1655, during the time of Chang, and operated continuously until the Chinese "Cultural Revolution" in 1966. The market was re-opened in 1984, and totally redone in the year 2000.

Francesca, Brenda, and I took a taxi from our hotel to the Night Market at about 8:00 PM. It was located near the eastern gate of the Imperial Palace in a bustling, trendy shopping area. The night was cold, but the streets were crowded with local people, and they were all eating the delicacies from the vendors. We were warned that the hygiene of the street market was questionable, but I still wanted to try some of the exotic cultural dishes they prepared.

The market had more than eighty stainless steel carts. Each cart had two gas burners and sported a red and white striped awning. The vendors were loud and competitive as each tried to convince you to buy their food items. One after another they would push their speared specialties into our faces. Everything you can imagine, and some you would never imagine, was there for you to buy and eat. All were carefully impaled on bamboo skewers.

Some of the more exotic food items that we were offered included scorpions, grasshoppers, silk worms (alive and wiggling), snakes, sea horses, and even starfish. In the midst of this culinary nightmare, I lost my courage for exotic foods and opted for what appeared to be a safe choice.

I ordered stuffed pot stickers on a stick. The man fried them up for me and I handed the stick to Francesca so she could try it.

After taking just two bites Francesca gave the skewer back to me and said, "I don't want this, you can have it."

I took the skewer from her and ate the entire thing. A few moments later Francesca informed me that the reason that she had given me the pot stickers was because she had found a long black hair in the last bite she ate.

Once Francesca shared her story about the pot stickers with me, we all opted to go to one of the very nice looking restaurants that line the street. The one we chose appeared very clean and was beautifully decorated in classic Chinese decor. This was not a tourist restaurant. The menus were not in English and no one there even spoke any English.

We decided to try to order from pictures in the menu, but the food was so exotic that we could not tell what it was. Finally, across the room we saw something familiar; it was a platter of chicken. We could tell because it was not cut up and had the form of a chicken. I motioned to a waitress and pointed to the tray of food across the room. Soon afterward she brought us our chicken.

When we were served our platter of chicken, we realized that there was something unusual about the garnish on it. As we looked closer, we realized it was not a garnish at all, but the severed head of the poor bird. Francesca placed a napkin over its head and then began to cut the rest of it for us. When we got the chicken on our plates and tried to eat it, we realized that it was cold and kind of raw. We did not speak enough Chinese however to complain about this.

"Maybe this is the way they eat it," I said.

"We really can't eat this," said Francesca.

None of us ate any of the food. We paid our bill and left the restaurant still hungry.

By this time, the stench of the things being cooked at the Night Market was overwhelming. I was beginning to feel nauseated.

"Let's get out of here. This place is making me sick," I said.

We quickly left the area of the night market and walked to a nearby shopping area. Here we found many small stores selling items of jade and strings of pearls along with numerous other souvenir items.

I had warned Francesca and Brenda, before we went out, to be careful with their belongings. I had locked most of my things in the safe in our room. The area around the night market is notorious for pickpockets. Francesca had left her purse in our room. I wore my wallet in a pouch around my neck.

As we walked through one extremely crowded gift store, Brenda yelled out, "Give me back my wallet!"

She grabbed a young man standing behind her and demanded that he give her possessions back. He only shrugged and shook his head. Brenda had been robbed. She had kept a wallet in her jacket pocket, despite my warnings, and someone in the store had taken advantage of her as an easy mark. She told the storeowners what had happened; they were polite, but not very helpful. Brenda was furious.

"How could Chang let this happen to me? First I fell down at the airport, and now I get pickpocketed. I really can't believe it," said Brenda angrily.

"Chang is like an angel, Brenda. He can't protect us from our free will," I said. "I warned you about this place before we left. We were very careful not to place anything of value where anyone could get it. You put your wallet in you jacket pocket. That was your choice. It was just too easy for them to resist."

"The wallet only had about $20 in it, but I also had all of my medical records in it. What am I going to do now?" Brenda said.

Francesca shook her head and said, "Brenda, why are you putting all this negativity out there? You know we are protected. You're not going to get sick. Maybe a pickpocket can get your wallet if you let him, and maybe you could fall at the airport, but Chang isn't going to let us get into any real trouble here. We're here for a reason and we're going to be okay."

We caught a taxi back, and then had a bite to eat at one of the fast-food restaurants that lined our hotel entrance. We had survived another adventure and learned still more important lessons.

❀ The Summer Palace

On Friday, October 16, we awoke early, ate breakfast together, and asked the concierge to write the name and directions to the Summer Palace in Chinese for us. We went to the front of our hotel and caught a cab. The cab ride took about thirty minutes and we were dropped off at the main entrance, at the east gate of the complex.

The Summer Palace covers over seven hundred acres. Kunming Lake, located in the center of the park, takes up most of these parklands. This was the summer residence of China's royal families for nearly eight hundred years.

This grand park is filled with beautiful courtyards and covered walkways. We purchased all-inclusive admissions so we could see as much of the park as possible. More than anything else, however, we were obsessed with looking for the multicolored butterfly that Chang told us about the night before.

We spent over four hours exploring the vast grounds and found only one small white butterfly that followed us up the giant pagoda called "The Tower of Fragrant Buddha." We took one of the Dragon Boats across the lake, and were about to leave the park through the entrance we came in, when I noticed something in one of my guidebooks that intrigued me. There was a restored shopping area once used by China's imperial family and their entourage called "Suzhou Street." The entire area was rebuilt in a classical Ming Dynasty style. All the shops sold wares from that era.

We realized from our map of the park that this shopping area was on the far side of the lake from us. We took another Dragon Boat to a spot near the point on the map that we were looking for. After some searching, we found the street. It was very fascinating and well worth the effort to find it. It was built on a narrow canal through which some of the waters diverted from the lake ran.

Francesca was overjoyed by the authentic articles from the era of Chinese royalty that were for sale there. She purchased a flowered crown headpiece based on the ones worn by princesses of the Ming and Qing Dynasties. She put it on and wore it. Her actions amused the Chinese tourists. Many laughed when they saw her with the headpiece on, and they even gave her an occasional "thumbs up" sign.

"Look, I'm a princess," she said jubilantly. "I think the people here recognize me."

We found another gate out of the Summer Palace near Suzhou Street, and proceeded to exit the park. As we did this, three short Chinese women in raggedy dresses came up to us, trying to sell us souvenir postcards. One of the women reached into her bag on the ground next to her, and pulled out a butterfly pressed in wax paper. "Ten yuan," she said in broken English.

"*Bo,*" I said to her, which translates to "no" in Chinese, waving my hand. The woman then began to unfurl all of the pressed butterflies from her bag. She stood up and let them fall in a long connected chain to the ground. There were about twenty different butterflies and they were all hooked together in their packages. These butterflies were all different colors. They were beautiful.

"*Bo! Bo!*" I shouted, trying to move the raggedy woman away from me.

Then it hit me, "Oh my God!" I said. "These are the butterflies that Chang told us about. This is the sign that we've been looking for all day. It's a sign to Francesca that her aunt is with us, just like he said she'd be. It's a sign that heaven is really near us all the time."

Francesca was overwhelmed by the event. She told me she wanted to purchase the swallowtail butterfly the woman was selling. I haggled with the woman, and purchased it for two yuan (about twenty cents) Francesca and I now keep it as proof that this miracle really did happen. During our two trips to China that year, we never saw anyone selling butterflies before or after this occurrence.

✸ The National Museum of China

On Monday, October 18, we decided to visit the National Museum of China. This museum was located about two miles from our hotel, across the street from Tiananmen Square. The museum is housed in a massive building. It contains a museum of Chinese History and the Museum of the Chinese Revolution. We were more interested in history than Communist propaganda, so we visited the Museum of Chinese History.

The museum was composed of three enormous floors connected by a large, wide, and steep stairway. There were no elevators and no escalators. The museum was said to contain China's largest collection of historical artifacts, including bronze items dating back to 3000 BC. All the exhibits were arranged in chronological order from the oldest to the newest. The first floor gallery had skeletons and pottery from the Stone Age site in Banpo, and artifacts from the Xia and Shang Dynasties, from 2100 to 1100 BC. It also had two terracotta warriors and a horse from the Qin Dynasty, and silks and pottery from the Tang Dynasty.

The second floor was even more interesting to us. It contained artifacts from the Kangxi period of the Qing Dynasty. Here they had some of China's national treasures, including jewelry and other items from the emperor's personal collection.

When we climbed the museum's stairway to the topmost level, we were surprised at what we found. Unlike the other musky and dusty parts of the museum, this floor was clean and very modern. It housed a high-tech wax museum, which was not mentioned in any of our guidebooks, yet it truly deserved to be.

We entered at the south side of the wax museum. There we found life-size figures of contemporary heroes. These included sports figures such as soccer star Pele and basketball greats Michael Jordan and Yao Ming. Other familiar faces in this museum were Charlie Chaplin, Marilyn Monroe, Ingrid Bergman, Picasso, and even Bill Gates.

As we left the south side of the wax museum, we were confronted by the Chinese history portion of the presentation. Here we first found a whole gang of Red Chinese revolutionaries, none of whom I had ever heard of, along with their leader Mao Zedong. As we ventured further, we saw wax figures of Confucius, Shi Huang of the Qin Dynasty, and Kublai Khan of the Yuan Dynasty.

Then, as we rounded a bend, I saw something that made my body tingle and the hair on my arms stand up. It was a life-size statue of the Kangxi Emperor of the Qing Dynasty. I recognized him right away. It was Chang, exactly as I see him in my meditations. He stood with his hand on his chin looking curiously at us. The painted background simulated his chambers in the Imperial Palace.

"Hi, Chang," I said with reverence.

I was happy and surprised to find him here. I stood and stared at this wax figure for several minutes, in awe of what I had discovered. It felt like I had found a long lost friend. Tears welled up in my eyes as I looked into his wise face.

Francesca, Brenda, and I spent about twenty minutes with Chang. We took photos and even talked to the wax figure. It was an amazing and overwhelming experience to feel like I was actually up close and face-to-face with my spirit guide on this plane of existence.

❀ The Lama Temple

On Tuesday, October 19, the three of us decided to visit the Lama Temple. We had heard that it was a bright spot in the vast dispirited wilderness of Beijing. During our first visit to China, Francesca and I had noted that there was a feeling of sadness wherever we went. It was like a void where all the spirit of the people had been sucked out and replaced by a cold, hollow feeling.

Francesca and I had visited Japan in November of 2003, and knew how spiritual that culture had felt to us. We had visited numerous Buddhist and Shinto temples in the cities of Kamakura and Tokyo. The representatives of my Japanese book company had also taught us how to properly conduct the rituals at the temples, how to receive our fortunes, and what to do if our fortune was positive or negative. Through doing this, we learned a new respect for the people and religions of Japan.

Unlike those in Japan, many of the major Buddhist temples in Beijing had been converted into museums. The Confucius Temple was mainly a museum, the Temple of Heaven, the Five Pagoda Temple, the White Pagoda Temple, and many others were now totally dispirited museums. We had nearly lost hope of finding anything spiritual at all in Beijing when we visited the Lama Temple.

The first indication that things were getting more spiritual came when we got to the part of town where the temple is located. The streets around it were lined with dozens of religious shops selling temple incense, Buddha beads, wind chimes, and numerous Buddhist icons.

The pungent smell of incense filled the air all around the temple, as we paid our admission and entered the massive complex. We were amazed by the beauty and spirituality we saw. The place was overflowing with frescos and tapestries.

We worked our way through the hundreds of prostrate followers of Tibetan Buddhism as we visited the five magnificent worship halls, all filled with amazing Tibetan Buddhist imagery. We were surprised to see dozens of the Buddhist monks praying and practicing their faith in each of the buildings. We later learned that more than two hundred monks live in the complex.

Francesca felt a particular fascination with this temple and the Tibetan Buddhism it espoused. At the entrance to every worship hall and shrine, she would kneel, place her head down all the way on the floor, and pray. She said that she felt connected to this temple and its religion. She believed that all of her prayers would be answered there. She said that it filled her heart with joy to know that faith and spirituality still existed in China.

Francesca was also excited to see the massive collection of religious items from Chang's collection. She was consoled to know that he felt the same way she did about religion. She knew that he had led her to this temple.

A highlight of the temple was a seventy-five-foot statue of Buddha carved from a single sandalwood tree. The worship hall that the statue was located inside of had actually been built around the giant statue itself. Buddha's head stuck out the top of the hall. This statue had been a big draw for pilgrims from throughout China, Tibet, and Mongolia for many years. It still enthralled the followers of Tibetan Buddhism the day we were there.

The Lama Temple is still so important that even in the midst of "Red" China, it is today considered one of the holiest Tibetan Buddhist Temples in the world. The majority of Dalai Lamas in this faith have been chosen in this temple. It is believed by many that the next Dalai Lama will be affirmed there as well.

The Lama Temple was originally built by Chang in 1694, as a residence for his son, Prince Yen Zhen, who would later become the emperor of China. In 1744, this palace was converted into a Tibetan Buddhist temple by the Qianlong emperor. This temple soon became the home of a multitude of Tibetan and Mongolian monks. The Qianlong emperor used the temple to maintain China's control over Mongolia and Tibet by training the religious leaders of Tibetan Buddhism to follow China's orders.

To end manipulation and dispute caused by the search for new Dalai Lamas, the Qianlong emperor came up with a method to determine the religious leadership. For this, he used a solid gold urn as a divination tool. He had the names and birth dates of the candidates for Dalai Lama written on ivory lots and put in the urn. Religious rituals were then held and the name of the real Dalai Lama was drawn from the urn. The person whose name was selected was made the Dalai Lama after the process was approved by the Chinese central government.

The fourteenth Dalai Lama was the first in over two hundred years to be chosen without the Chinese lottery system described above. He was given an exemption from the then–Republic of China to be allowed not to use the traditional lottery system, granted by a special decree. It is very likely that the Chinese lottery method will be used to choose the fifteenth Dalai Lama.

We were not brainwashed by tour guides or Chinese government handlers during this trip to Beijing; we did everything on our own. We saw something truly spiritual and wonderful happening at the Lama Temple.

There were a huge number of people worshiping there. I could feel their sincerity of purpose. This experience has made me more optimistic about the future of spirituality in China.

❀ The Return of the Empress

Our friend Brenda was becoming very discouraged about what was happening to her during our trip. When we returned to our hotel from the Lama Temple, she seemed more upset than ever. We had planned to go to the Beijing Opera that night, but she was now feeling too sick to accompany us.

Brenda came to our room and said, "I can't believe all of the bad luck I've had on this trip so far. First I fell down and hurt my knee, then I got jostled by that crazy cab driver, then they robbed me at the Night Market, and now I'm sick with a stomach virus. What's going to happen to me next?"

"Brenda, I don't think any of the things that have happened to you so far have occurred by accident," I said. "This looks like something that Sylvia Browne calls 'site energy.' I learned about this while researching reincarnation for the angel classes at our store. Site energy is a phenomenon that affects a certain place like a haunted house or places where someone lived in a past life. It affects people a lot of different ways. Some people have dizzy spells and others get sick. Many people are prone to accidents when they first come into contact with this energy."

"So, what does this have to do with me?" asked Brenda.

"When we came to Beijing last March, Francesca fell down on her face the first day we got here and got a black eye. Like you, she was reacting to a lower frequency of energy from her past life that still lingers in Beijing. All the bad things that are happening to you are just proof that you've lived here in a past life too."

"That's all well and good," said Brenda, "But I'd really like to go to the Beijing Opera tonight. Could you meditate and talk to Chang about healing me? If this is all karmic, like you say, Chang should be able to do something about it."

"Let me see what I can do," I said as I sat down on the couch in the room, closed my eyes, and meditated. About a minute later, I saw Chang standing before me. "Can you help Brenda?" I asked.

"Yes," Chang nodded. "I can see that she has allowed spiders and scorpions to get into her body."

"Can you please take them out of her?" I asked.

"Of course," Chang said. "If she lets me do it."

I came out of my meditation and told Brenda the situation. "Would you mind if Chang takes the spiders and scorpions out of you?"

"Of course he may," replied Brenda.

I then went back into meditation. "Chang, Brenda says that it's okay to heal her."

Chang then reached into Brenda and pulled out the spiders and scorpions. As the insects came out of her they appeared to vanish into thin air. After about a minute, Chang made a gesture to let me know he had finished healing Brenda.

Brenda sat on the couch for a few moments and then returned to her room and rested. About an hour later she came back to our room and told us she felt much better. We all went downstairs to the lobby and had a hotel representative hail a taxi for us to a local Beijing Opera theater.

The Beijing Opera is something very different than the Western concept of opera. It consists of morality plays and Chinese mythical stories portrayed by people with brightly painted faces and masks. The opera includes singing, dancing, choreographed fight scenes, and even martial arts demonstrations.

The concept of the opera goes back over eight hundred years. It originated as shows performed by touring troupes of singers and dancers. In the seventeenth century, Chang officially sanctioned the Beijing Opera as an art form and set up theaters in Beijing for its performances.

We arrived at the theater early and found it to be nearly empty. The hostess, a pretty young Chinese woman in traditional costume, came to seat us. The room was full of round tables with chairs around them. She led us to a table in a dark rear corner of the theater. We were not happy with our seating assignment.

"Can we have a better table than this? There are lots of empty tables up front," Brenda protested.

The young Chinese woman shook her head and said, "If I place you in one of those tables you'll have to share it with another couple."

"Put us up there. We're always happy to meet new friends." I insisted.

"All right, if that is what you want. Follow me," she said.

She led us to a table near the front center section of the theater. This was a great location and we quickly sat down and sipped the tea and sampled the snacks that were brought to our table.

A few moments later, the hostess returned with a young Chinese couple to share our table. At first we were a little shy as we all smiled awkwardly at each other. Then the Chinese man spoke to us in very good English. "Hello, my name is Tak and this is my wife Monica."

I introduced myself to them and remarked on their excellent English.

"We're from Hong Kong," said Tak. "My wife and I are here on vacation."

"Where are you staying?" I asked.

"Oh, we're staying at the Courtyard by Marriott," replied Tak.

I was dumbstruck. "What are the odds of this? There are about one thousand hotels in Beijing and we are seated with a couple who are bilingual Chinese/English staying at the same hotel as us," I thought. "We're staying at the Marriott too," I said enthusiastically.

"Maybe you can help me," said Tak. "Tomorrow, Monica and I are planning to visit the Great Wall. Do you know of any good tours we could take?"

We had been planning a trip to the Great Wall the next day ourselves. "I know of a great tour and we'd like to go with you," I said. "I found it in one of my guide books of Beijing. The tour is made for local tourists. It's all in Chinese and leaves from Tiananmen Square. It goes to places the English-speaking tours don't go and it costs much less money. We could only go on a tour like this with people like you who speak both English and Chinese."

Tak seemed impressed by my research of Chinese tours. He looked at Monica and she nodded excitedly. "We'd love to go with you," he said.

We all enjoyed the Beijing Opera together and when it ended we returned to our hotel and all got a good night's sleep.

Francesca and I awoke at 7:00 AM and Brenda knocked at our door a short time later. We all went down to the hotel restaurant and met Tak and Monica for breakfast. After breakfast, we headed out of our hotel to a subway station about two blocks away. We had not taken the subway before, due to our limited knowledge of Chinese. We were afraid that we might get lost and never find our way back again.

Tak and Monica were experts at the Beijing subway system. They took us right to the correct train and knew the station where we had to get off. The price to take the subway was about the same as a taxi ride, but the trip was a lot quicker and safer. We made it to our station at Tiananmen Square in less than five minutes.

Finding the tour bus we were looking for, however, was not as easy as it had seemed from my guide book. There were hundreds of buses coming in and out of this enormous area. To make things even more complicated, there were dozens of young men and women wearing I.D. cards on strings around their necks trying to sell bus tours. We were looking for a green bus with a number "1" in its name plate. All the buses were green, so it was really confusing.

Finally Tak found a female tour representative who claimed to be with the bus we were looking for. She led us to the correct bus and we paid to get on and had to pay another fee for the tour. This was still quite economical and only came to about 250 yuan ($25) each.

When we finally got seated I looked at Tak and said, "Where is our tour going today?"

Tak shook his head, a little embarrassed, and said, "I'm really not sure. We're going to the Great Wall, the Ming Tombs, and a lot of other places too. It even includes lunch."

I laughed and said, "Well Tak, it looks like we're just going to have to go with the flow and just enjoy this trip as another adventure."

Our bus left Tiananmen Square about 9:00 AM and headed off to the part of the Great Wall called the Badaling Wall. Francesca and I had visited it in March and I really was not that excited to visit it again. The Chinese tour, however, was different. Instead of just being let off the bus for an hour to explore the Wall, we were given tickets to ride a bobsled-like devise up the wall on a conveyor belt and then coast back down to the bottom again.

This was a somewhat dangerous way to see the wall. There were no seat belts or restraints of any kind. You just had to hang on for your life. All of us took the bobsleds and surprisingly we all had a really great time riding them and exploring the Wall together.

After an hour on the Wall, we returned to our bus and headed off for destinations unknown. We first visited a jade factory. Our friend Tak warned us not to buy anything there because the jade was way overpriced. From the jade factory, we walked to a typical Chinese restaurant where we all shared plates of vegetables and a large whole fish. With Tak and Monica's help, we were able to communicate with all the people at our table. We found that this was their first time to Beijing. They were from cities all over China. Many of them had never even met an American before. I felt that this was a good opportunity to improve relations between the United States and China. We all ate together and left the table as good friends.

From the restaurant our bus took us to a sort of theme park called "Old Beijing." This replica of Beijing in the seventeenth century included old buildings that were moved to this site and repaired to show off their former grandeur during the Qing Dynasty. In some ways this town reminded me of Knott's Berry Farm, a theme park in Southern California, which depicts a nineteenth century town from the Old West.

Old Beijing even had a gambling hall and a house of prostitution. While there, we were treated to a performance that reminded me of a circus side show in which people pounded nails into their noses and swallowed and then regurgitated large metal balls.

From Old Beijing our bus took us to a dry goods store where you could buy various dried fruits and candies, as well as Beijing-style ducks that were being cooked assembly-line style in a large wooden oven. After this, we went to a traditional Chinese medicine clinic where we were all diagnosed and prescribed traditional herbal remedies. Tak again warned us here that we were being taken advantage of. He said the prices of the medicines prescribed were too high.

Our final destination of the bus tour was the Ming Tombs. We again visited the tomb of Zhu Di, the first emperor of the Ming Dynasty, which Francesca and I had visited in March. It was at this tomb that we had gained the clues that led us to know the true identity of Chang.

When we got there we found the tomb's parking lot was packed with tour buses full of Chinese tourists. As we explored the tomb complex, I noticed that something unusual was happening. Everywhere we went, hoards of Chinese tourists would follow us. They were not interested in Francesca and me at all. They were interested in Brenda. Brenda is a tall, sturdy, blond woman in her early sixties. There appeared to be something unusual about her that was attracting these Chinese people.

"Keith, what's going on here?" said Brenda. "Why are all of these people following us?"

"I think they want to take pictures with you," I said.

Brenda walked over to a man who was now leading the crowd of people in our entourage. He pointed to his camera and nodded his head. Brenda nodded her head in acceptance. The man then had his wife and family stand with Brenda and took their photos. After this, the people just lined up and one after another had their photos taken with Brenda.

We walked back to our bus and were greeted by more Chinese tourists, all of whom wanted to see Brenda. Brenda walked over to the tour bus next to ours and the people cheered when she entered it. She finally left the neighboring bus and returned to our bus and we left for downtown Beijing.

On our way back, Brenda turned to me and said, "What happened at the Ming Tombs today? That was really weird. With all those people flocking around me, I felt like I was an empress or something."

"Brenda, I think there's something about the 'site energy' at the Ming Tombs that caused that to occur. Did you notice that people in our tour didn't care about you, but all the other tourists on the other buses did?" I said.

"Yeah, why did that happen? I thought that was really weird," said Brenda.

"I think that the people on our tour had been exposed to your energy for several hours and were probably immune to you. The tourists at the Ming Tombs were hit by your energy along with the 'site energy' that exists there and on some level of consciousness knew who you were," I replied.

"So who was I?" pleaded Brenda.

"Don't you remember? You are the empress from the seventeenth century who's finally returned to her people in China," I said. "These people probably don't know why, but they feel that they know you and they want to be with you."

"I'm confused about something," said Brenda. "If I was a Qing empress from the seventeenth century, why would the 'site energy' at a fourteenth century Ming Tomb affect me?"

"From what I've read about site energy," I said, "there are no bounds to it. It's like some sort of vortex or something. Once you get into it, this energy just opens everything and people have past-life experiences and become aware of their life missions. It can really be a confusing experience when you encounter this force."

"Why was I the only one affected at the Ming Tombs? Why didn't the crowds of tourists follow you and Francesca and want to take their pictures with you too?" asked Brenda.

"I don't know," I replied. "Maybe we just weren't as famous or don't have as powerful an energy as you do. I think we'll find out more when we visit the Qing Tombs tomorrow."

Our friends Tak and Monica were amazed by the day's events. They told us they had never seen anything like this happen before. They were at a loss for words over how Brenda had attracted such a large following of Chinese tourists at the Ming Tombs.

❀ The Qing Tombs

On Thursday, October 21, we again woke up early and finally made our long-awaited trek to the Qing Tombs. These tombs are seventy-eight miles from downtown Beijing. It took us four hours to get there. They are located just beyond the municipal border at the town of Malanyu in Zunhua County. The Qing Tombs are not a popular tourist destination, and are seldom visited by Westerners.

There are no organized tours to this remote site, so we contacted our hotel's concierge, who arranged for us to hire a driver. The driver and car cost one thousand yuan (about $100) for the day. We also paid road tolls and an entry fee to visit the tomb complex.

We had learned from our research that the Qing Tombs had been open to the public for less than twenty years. This complex was used by the Qing royalty from 1633 to 1935. It contains fifteen tombs, they hold the remains of five emperors, fifteen empresses, three princes, two princesses and 136 concubines, as well as the Kangxi Emperor's (or Chang's) teacher.

The tombs form a countryside version of the Imperial Palace. The location for these tombs was determined by Emperor Shunzhi, the founder of the Qing Dynasty (Chang's father), who discovered this valley during a hunting trip. These tombs today make up China's largest dynastic cemetery.

The Qing Tombs were placed in this remote location due to its perfect *feng shui*. The valley that they are in is protected from natural elements and is believed to screen off the threat of evil forces, both from the front and the rear. The mountain ranges in the remote valley form a perfect protective screen for the tombs. A mountain peak to the south is said to protect the dead from the wind. Hills to the east and west also stand guard.

To this day, many Chinese people regard the Qing Tombs as being in a cosmically fortified location. The tombs have never been harmed by natural disasters such as floods or droughts. One very unusual fact about this area is that it rains exactly seventy-two times each year, no more and no less.

In 1976, an earthquake that destroyed the city of Tangshan, just sixty miles away, and killed over 250,000 people, caused no damage to the Qing Tombs. This is truly a sacred and blessed final resting place for the royalty of China.

The driver who took us to the tombs spoke pretty fluent English. We were excited to know that we had someone to explain the complex and its inhabitants to us. When we finally arrived at our destination, we were all extremely disappointed when our driver said, "I don't do tombs. I'm not going with you."

Our driver found a guide for us: a small Chinese man who appeared to be in his late twenties. He said his name was Yen Su, and then he motioned for us to enter the wagon he pulled behind his rickshaw. He spoke no English. We were all very disappointed to have him as our tour guide for the Qing Tombs.

Our rickshaw was actually a motor scooter, which shot black smelly smoke into our faces. Our wagon was made of wood and had a padded board placed across it for us to sit on. We found ourselves in the awkward position of trying to take a tour with only our hand gestures and our really bad Chinese to communicate with. We spent most of our time choking on exhaust fumes and trying not to fall out of the wagon as it traversed the rocky dirt trails around the tombs.

During our tour, we visited several of the Qing emperors' tombs. The most spectacular of these was that of Yu Ling. This tomb had been broken into and robbed in the early twentieth century. This was bad for Yu Ling, but good for us because it was open for visitors to see the burial chambers within it.

The tomb had nine elaborately decorated vaults, located 177 feet below the ground. The main vault had a large domed ceiling. On the ceiling of the chamber was carved the images of ten thousand Buddhas. This, we had found, was a sacred number that symbolized heaven. There were also thirty Tibetan scriptures carved into the walls, two three-ton marble doors with reliefs of Bodhisattvas (Enlightened Ones) and four protective kings engraved upon them.

The coffins of the emperor and his empresses had been rudely opened and looted. Several of these had been repaired and placed back into their proper places. Others were so badly broken that they had been moved out of the tomb. We were informed that for an extra charge, we could see the mummy of one of the empresses that had been removed from the tomb. We declined the opportunity to view this grizzly sight.

For us, however, our true mission was to visit Chang's tomb. We found it was relatively modest compared to the others in the complex. This was not surprising to me, because I had gotten to know him over the past few years, and knew the type of person he was.

Brenda and I had come to the tomb complex in casual hiking clothes. Francesca, however, had dressed up especially for her visit. She wore a beautiful golden Chinese silk blouse, with numerous butterflies embossed on it. She began to cry as we arrived outside the tomb's entrance.

When we walked through the entrance of the complex, we found to our surprise that we were the only tourists there. The only other people we saw were guards. They sat around playing cards and talking with each other.

On entering, we saw a five-arched marble bridge with guardian figures carved on it. We walked to the rear of the complex and found, to our disappointment, that the entrance to the burial vault was sealed with a thick steel chain and a large iron padlock. Francesca had hoped to leave a gift for Chang in the tomb. Her gift was to be a butterfly pin, like the one that came to our store seemingly by mistake by one of our vendors several months before.

We walked back in disappointment into the great offertory temple outside the tomb. I was amazed to find that the room was quite stark. It appeared that many of the items of value had been stolen or taken out for safekeeping.

The only highlight of the chamber was a throne area in its center. There stood nine great chairs. The most magnificent of these thrones was Chang's priceless Ceremonial Dragon Throne. These thrones were blocked from public access by large red velvet ropes. They were also surrounded by a swarm of high tech alarms and motion sensor devices.

Francesca became obsessed by being so close to the remains of her past-life father. She pulled her golden butterfly brooch out of her purse and said, "I've gotta give this to my Baba."

Before Brenda and I could stop her, she crawled under the velvet ropes like a rabbit. Ignoring the numerous motion sensors and alarms, she bounded over to Chang's Ceremonial Dragon Throne. There, she raised the satin cushion and placed her butterfly brooch beneath it. As Francesca did this, she set off many motion sensor alarms in the temple. The cushion fell to the floor and Francesca went back to put it back on the throne. This set off even more alarms.

A sense of foreboding and terror struck me as Francesca crawled back under the velvet ropes to the main walkway in the room. Looking out of the temple doors, I could see the guards from the tomb entrance about 100 yards in the distance. They were running our way. A vision of a Chinese prison came into my brain.

"Oh my God, what's Francesca done now?" I thought to myself.

We all quickly exited the offertory temple. There was no way out except for the entrance where the guards were coming from. We retreated to a point behind the temple, back to the locked gate of Chang's tomb.

"Keith! You've got to contact Baba," yelled Francesca. "He's the only one who can help us now."

"She's right, Keith. We're really in big trouble. We need Chang's help now," Brenda shouted.

I was very distracted, but I tried to quiet my mind. I began to breathe deeply and I visualized the stairway leading to the lush green meadow. At the tenth step, I reached the meadow and walked down a beautiful path with multicolored wildflowers blooming on each side of it. At the end of the path, I saw a waterfall and a large blue pond. Chang stood patiently, waiting for me, at the edge of the pond.

"Keith, it's so nice to see you. Thank you for visiting my cocoon," he said.

"Chang, we're in a lot of trouble!" I said. "Francesca has just set off the motion sensors in your offertory chamber. The guards are on their way to arrest us."

Chang looked at me calmly and said, "Tell my little butterfly thank you for the beautiful gift she left me."

"Francesca brought two butterfly brooches with her, one for you and the other for her mother from her past life in China. Francesca was concerned that she had only left one of the brooches at the offertory chamber." I replied.

"Tell her I love her and that I'll always love her. I'll tell her mother that the gift is for the two of us to share," said Chang. "Don't worry, the guards won't harm you. They won't even see you. They'll think that their equipment has just malfunctioned."

I came back from my meditation, unconvinced of our safety. The guards were still advancing. They were heading right toward us. Then, to my surprise, instead of coming after us, they walked into the offertory chamber. After a moment they walked out, shaking their heads, and grumbling something in Chinese. They did not even look in our direction. Then they all walked slowly back to their posts at the tomb complex entrance.

Francesca, Brenda, and I set down on a wall in front of the locked tomb, relieved by our narrow escape. Francesca then looked at me and said, "While we're here, can you ask Chang some more questions?"

I really was not in the mood to do another meditation, but the thought of having to pass through the temple guard posts again and risk arrest kept me planted on the wall. "Okay," I agreed. "Let's wait here a few minutes. Maybe the guards will forget about what happened and let us go, if we let this die down a little bit more."

I again did my meditation ritual. To my relief Chang was still there.

"Do you have any other messages for us?" I asked.

Chang looked at me solemnly, and said with a warm kindness in his dark brown eyes: "I am now standing just three feet away from you. I hope you are all satisfied that you have reached my tomb. I still wonder why you would want to visit my cocoon when you already have the butterfly. My tomb has never been robbed, so you couldn't have entered it. I assure you it is much more beautiful than Yu Ling's tomb that you just visited."

Francesca then asked Chang, "Have any of my brothers or sisters from our life in the seventeenth century ever visited your tomb?"

"Many of them have visited this tomb, but you were the first one to find out who you were," replied Chang.

"Chang, are we all buried in this tomb with you?" I asked.

Chang shook his head slowly and smiled as he answered. "You and Brenda are buried with me. You, Keith, were my teacher. Brenda was one of my empresses. We will always be connected as long as my tomb remains unopened. The others in my tomb are earthbound spirits. They are still stuck in my tomb with our cocoons. I am happy to see that you and Brenda have escaped to work out your karma in this lifetime."

"Where's Francesca cocoon? Isn't she in with us too?" I asked.

Chang shook his head, looked at me sadly, and said, "Francesca's not here. She's not buried with us. It broke my heart to lose her, but I traded her for peace."

"What do you mean?" I asked, now feeling very confused.

Chang looked downward in sadness, and said, "China needed peace, so I married Francesca to a prince from Mongolia."

When I relayed this message to Brenda and Francesca, they were both shocked. We had believed that we were all buried together in the Qing Tombs of China. Now we were sad to find that Francesca was not with us.

This revelation did not make any sense to me at all. I believed that the Qing rulers were too racially prejudiced to allow one of their princesses to marry outside of the Manchurian bloodline. Furthermore, why would the most powerful person on earth, Chang, be forced to marry his daughter to someone to achieve peace?

Francesca then asked a final question of Chang, "Did I go to your funeral when you died?"

I went back into meditation and asked Chang this question. He looked at me sadly and said, "No. I am sorry, but after I sent her to Mongolia, I never saw my little butterfly again."

After this session with Chang, we all decided to leave the tomb complex. We walked quickly past the entrance gate where the tomb guards stood. They viewed us with indifference. We then went to our rickshaw driver, who was waiting for us outside the complex. I motioned him to take us back to our driver. We got in the car and had a long, uneventful journey back to our hotel.

CHAPTER TWELVE

Butterfly Lovers Reunited

OUR TRIP TO BEIJING HAD been life changing. We were amazed by the experiences we had shared together. On Sunday, October 24, 2004, Francesca, Brenda, and I sadly prepared to leave Beijing.

We had spent eleven days and ten nights in this exciting city. The weather had been perfect during our entire trip, but we noticed on going outside of our hotel that the sky was now dark and foreboding. Light rain had already started, and we could hear muffled claps of thunder roaring in the distance.

✿ The Cab Ride Back

The doorman at our hotel opened an umbrella, and let us stand under it as he waved down a cab to take us to the airport. The taxi he summoned was a brand new, four-door Audi sedan, with plenty of room for the three of us and our bags. Unlike most of the cabs we had taken in Beijing, this car was big, clean, and comfortable.

The cab driver spoke broken English as we rode to the airport. "Winter come early to Beijing this year," he said. "Look like bad storm today."

"We've been here ten days and the weather has been pretty good. I guess we timed our trip very well," I replied.

The rain now began to pour down like a waterfall, and lightning flashed in front of us like strobe lights. We felt that Beijing was sad to see us leave, and was giving us this storm as a sign.

Our driver turned his windshield wipers on full blast and slowed down on the now rain-soaked roadway. The people usually drive pretty crazily in Beijing, but this storm was so bad that cars were pulling over to the side of the road to wait for it to subside.

"I hope we make it to airport," said our driver.

"Oh, don't worry, we're protected," I said. "We've been through a lot since we got to Beijing, and I know we are going to be all right."

Our driver drove on slowly, but we still arrived at the Beijing International Airport with plenty of time to spare. We ran from the cab through the pouring rain into the terminal.

❀ The Storm at the Terminal

By now, the storm was hitting the airport with its full force. The thunder rocked us like a cannon attack, even inside the terminal. Whenever a close strike hit, the lights flickered.

I looked at the electronic flight schedules and found that some of the outgoing flights had already been delayed by this act of God. We hoped that our flight would be able to make it out in this storm.

We found the line for our flight and received our tickets. We then went through the international customs area, where we were supposed to pay an airport tax. Somehow this was never assessed on us. The customs officials just stamped our passports and ripped out our visa papers and then let us go right into the terminal.

We went to the gate to board our flight. We could see through the terminal window that the storm was now hitting the airport even harder than before.

"Is this flight going to get off on time?" I asked the young woman at the flight desk.

"We don't know," she said. "This storm is really bad."

We took seats outside our boarding area and waited to see what would happen. The lightning continued to attack the airport with relentless vigor. It was announced that our boarding would be delayed by twenty minutes due to the storm.

Finally, an airline representative announced on the intercom that passengers on our flight were now allowed to board. We walked down the entryway and into the airplane.

❀ True Love Revealed

As we took our seats, a voice came over the intercom. "Good morning, passengers! This is the captain speaking. Due to the severity of the storm outside, flight control has informed me that we will have to delay our takeoff for at least another hour."

"It looks like we're going to be here for a while," I told Francesca, who was sitting next to me.

Francesca did not answer me. I then noticed that she was crying. At first she just whimpered like a lost child, but after a few moments, tears started running down her cheeks like a rain-swollen stream. She wiped the torrent of tears away, put her hands over her face, and continued to sob.

My first thought was that she was sad to be leaving Beijing for the second time in less than a year. Francesca seemed too upset for this to be her problem. She appeared to be releasing welled up feelings from the deepest depths of her soul. I have been with her for over thirty years, and I have never seen her as distressed as she was at that moment.

"What's the matter, my love? Why are you crying?" I asked. "Are you sad to be leaving Beijing?"

"No, Keith, that's not it at all," she said. "I'm crying because I've finally learned something that I should have known all along. Baba has shown me that you are the true love of my life."

"What do you mean?" I asked.

"Baba separated us three hundred years ago, and we've been trying to get back together ever since during our past lives," she said. "Up until now, we've always failed for one reason or another. When we left Beijing in March, I was planning to leave you. If our grandson Kyler hadn't been stillborn, and Keith and Leah hadn't moved in with us, I would have left you two years ago."

"What did you want to do if you left me?" I asked.

"I wanted to spend the rest of my life doing something meaningful. I wanted to become a nun. I've wanted to become a nun since I was a little girl. I tried to become one when I was a teenager, but my parents wouldn't let me. I felt pressured by my parents to get married and have grandchildren for them. That's why I married you."

"Why did you want to leave me?" I asked. "I just can't understand why you would want to do this."

"I didn't think that you loved me," Francesca said sadly.

"Why didn't you think I loved you?" I asked, now feeling very hurt.

"Keith, you really don't get it, do you?" she said.

"I guess I don't. Please explain the problem to me," I said.

"For the past ten years, all you've thought about is running our store and writing your books," said Francesca. "You would run our store twenty-four hours a day, seven days a week, if I let you. Also, when we come home at night, you don't want to be with me. You just want to lock yourself in your office and write and re-write your books."

"I didn't know you felt this way. I'm really sorry," I said humbly.

"Keith, please forgive me. Now I understand that your mission is to write the books you're so obsessed with. You have to keep writing your books because everyone in the world has to know about Baba. He has shown me that you are my true love. That's why I'm crying. Our life mission has finally become clear to me. It's kind of like the vows you read in the ring ceremony in the weddings that you perform. True love is something eternal. It can never end."

"What do you mean by that?"

"What I mean," Francesca answered, "is that between March and today I've come to realize that Baba's messages are real. He's trying to show us something that we both need to do."

"What is Chang trying to tell us?" I asked, still confused.

"He's trying to tell us both that our love is very important to him. I am your true love and you are my true love too. Baba said that truth will set me free, and now I know what he means," she said.

"What does he mean?" I asked.

"He means that we have been brought together in this lifetime for a reason. We have shared many lives together and never fulfilled our spiritual destiny. When Baba sent me to Mongolia, it broke my heart, it broke your heart, and it broke his heart too."

"I get it now," I said. "I was such a fool. I was given the gift of true love and I have taken it for granted all these years."

Chang always says that some people find their true love and they let them go. I now knew that I had come close to losing Francesca again in this lifetime. Chang had come to me to save my marriage. He had come to help Francesca and me fulfill our karmic destinies.

The captain again came on the intercom, "Good morning, passengers! Flight control has informed me that the storm has now subsided enough for us to prepare for takeoff. Please fasten your seatbelts and put all your belongings either under your seats or in the overhead bin."

A few moments later, our plane roared down the runway and climbed high into the clouds far above the bustling city of Beijing. Francesca and I held hands and smiled at each other as our plane climbed above the raging storm. We could feel our hearts dancing happily, like two beautiful golden butterflies, as we flew together into the heavens. We both knew that this was how we should have left China three hundred years before.

More Secrets Revealed

WHEN WE ARRIVED BACK IN the United States, Francesca and I realized that there were still some unanswered questions about our past lives in seventeenth-century China. The two most important questions that we needed to address were: Why was the Butterfly Princess sent to marry a prince from Mongolia? And why was I, a Chinese commoner, buried in the tomb with the great Kangxi Emperor and his royal family?

✸ Galdan Khan

I found, through extensive computer and library research, that Chang's revelation of the fate of the Butterfly Princess was one hundred percent correct. In 1690, Chang embarked upon a major campaign to reunify China. His main objective was to reclaim the Mongolian territories held by Kublai Khan in the thirteenth century.

This was especially important to Chang because the Mongolians to the north of him had ambitions of their own. They made no secret of their plans to take over all of the known world, as they had under the rule of Genghis Khan in the thirteenth century. Their first objective was to take back all the lands they had previously held, from the Khingan Mountains of Siberia to the Volga River of Europe.

In 1691, Chang sent a large regiment of soldiers to confront Mongolian leader Prince Galdan Khan (also known as Khan Gordhun), and his armies. To Chang's great embarrassment, his troops were defeated by the Mongolians. This defeat put China and the Qing Dynasty in great danger.

In an effort to save China from a bloody war and to bring about a peace treaty with the Mongolians, Chang sent his sixteen-year-old daughter Bochita, whom he called "Butterfly," to marry the forty-six-year-old Galdan Khan. This was something Chang would regret later in that lifetime, and would play itself out in the karma of many other lifetimes.

Galdan Khan was the youngest of twelve sons of the Mongolian leader Baatar Khongtaiji. He was also the grandson of Gushi Khan, the Mongolian ruler who had placed the fourth Dalai Lama in power in Tibet. He was born in 1645. As was the custom of those times, his father decided that Galdan, as his youngest son, should be a Buddhist monk. At the age of six, Galdan was sent to Tibet for religious training.

Galdan's life in Tibet appears to have been a pleasant one. Being the son of the most powerful Mongolian of his time, he was soon granted many titles and high positions. The most important of these positions was being recognized as the incarnate Lama of Wensa Monastery. Galdan trained there under the fourth and fifth Dalai Lamas. In 1668, he was given the highest title of the Tibetan Buddhist religion, Boshughtu (blessed king), by the fifth Dalai Lama.

In 1671, Galdan Khan left the monastery in Tibet and returned to Mongolia to avenge the murder of his brother Sengge, who had been killed in a battle between feuding Mongolian warlords. His success in these battles led him to be acclaimed as a great leader of the Mongolian people.

Due to Galdan Khan's power as a secular and religious leader of the Mongolians, his marriage to the Butterfly Princess did not end his battles with China. He headed a civil war in Mongolia and became the first man to gain complete control of the Mongolian nation since Genghis Khan.

In 1696, Galdan Khan began a Mongolian campaign to conquer the world. Like Genghis Khan, he planned to attack China first. Seeing the threat posed by Galdan Khan, Chang sent 80,000 troops to crush his forces. Galdan Khan and his armies were defeated near present day Ulaanbaatar, just two hundred miles north of Beijing. Due to this defeat, Mongolia came under the rule of China. Galdan Khan retreated to Tibet, where he committed suicide the following year.

Chang's defeat of Galdan Khan is considered by many to be his greatest victory. It saved both China and the Western world from Galdan Khan's marauding army. The Mongolian forces had planned to conqueror Europe once they had defeated China. For the next 150 years, after Chang conquered the Mongolians, no foreign army would attack China.

After I told her this historical information, confirming Chang's messages about the Butterfly Princess, Francesca was overwhelmed with emotion and began to cry. She still had more questions for me, however.

✿ Exiled in Tibet

"What happened to me? What happened to the Butterfly Princess then?" pleaded Francesca.

"I don't know," I said. "There's nothing in the Chinese history texts I've read about what happened to Emperor Kangxi's daughter after she was sent to Mongolia. I'll keep looking if you like."

"Keith, could you please talk to Baba and see if he can tell you what happened to me?" Francesca said, sobbing.

Seeing her in such a sad and depressed state, I could not turn her down. "I'll see what I can do," I said.

I quieted my mind and began my meditation. Before long, Chang was standing before me.

"It's always nice to see you, Keith," he said. "You've learned a lot about me and your past life in China in the last few months. Why do you keep looking these things up in books? Don't you believe what I'm telling you?"

"It's not that I don't believe you, Chang, it's just that I'm writing a book about this, and I think it will make it all more credible if I can reference sources, other that you, for its content," I said.

"Why have you come to talk with me today?" he asked.

"The reason I'm here is that I've come to a dead end in the historical texts. I would like to know what happened to the Butterfly Princess after the death of Galdan Khan. Francesca is really concerned about this. "

"I would never want to upset my little butterfly," said Chang. "I know the rest of the story, and I will tell it to you now."

"The Butterfly Princess was married to Galdan Khan from 1691 to 1697. During this time, she had just one child by Galdan. The child died shortly after it was born. My little butterfly was just twenty-three years old when Galdan died. Since she had no living children or relatives in Mongolia, she was sent to live out the rest of her life as a Buddhist nun in a Tibetan convent. There, her head was shaved and she was taught the ways of Tibetan Buddhism," Chang explained. "My little butterfly was given high status and prestige at the monastery. She was both the widow of the renowned Mongolian prince Galdan Khan and the daughter of the world's most powerful emperor. The Butterfly Princess became a confidant of the sixth Dalai Lama, Tsangyang Cyatso, and it was with her help that Tibetan Buddhism became established as the main religion of China."

"Everything you've told me is really interesting, but I'm a little confused about something," I said. "Didn't you tell me at your tomb in China that the Butterfly Princess was buried in Mongolia? Now you're saying she ended up in Tibet."

Chang looked at me, shook his head, smiled, and said, "Keith, don't you know anything about geography? In those days Tibet was in Mongolia."

Then Chang said something very interesting, something I would never have thought of, or even considered. "Keith, in your lifetime you have what they call the fourteenth Dalai Lama. By our traditional beliefs, all Dalai Lamas are in a direct line of reincarnation from the great Buddha. Since Francesca knew the sixth and seventh Dalai Lamas in this past life, your current Dalai Lama (the fourteenth) will probably recognize her if he sees her."

This conversation with Chang inspired me to do more research. I found that the Butterfly Princess had come to Tibet in a very unique period in the history of Tibetan Buddhism. The fifth Dalai Lama, Ngawang Lozang Gyatso, had died in 1682.

His successor, the sixth Dalai Lama, was considered to be such an embarrassment to the religious and secular leaders of Tibet that they had kept the death of the fifth Dalai Lama a secret. The sixth Dalai Lama was said to spend most of his time conducting sexual orgies and writing erotic poetry. The government of Tibet was in total disarray due to this Dalai Lama's neglecting of his political and religious responsibilities.

After learning of this problem with the sixth Dalai Lama, I again meditated and met with Chang. I knew I had to ask him many questions.

"Chang, why would your daughter want to associate with the sixth Dalai Lama? That guy was bad news," I said.

Chang looked at me solemnly and replied, "My little butterfly was my most spiritual daughter and I loved her very much. She accepted her fate without question or complaint. By doing what she did, she saved Tibetan Buddhism."

"How did that happen?" I asked.

Chang shook his head, ran his fingers through his beard and said, "The death of the fifth Dalai Lama and the disaster that happened with the sixth Dalai Lama had been hidden from me for fifteen years. My little butterfly secretly sent me a message from her convent in Tibet that told me about this problem."

"How could she send you a message from Tibet?" I asked.

"I had a financial minister that I would send to Tibet to make sure they were paying the proper tribute to me," said Chang. "I used him to send messages to my little butterfly and to take messages back to me."

"Is our friend Vicki the reincarnation of this minister?" I asked.

"Yes," said Chang. "She was the one that sent the messages. Vicki is still part of your soul group now, isn't she?"

"Yes, she is," I nodded. "So what happened when you received the message from the Butterfly Princess about the Dalai Lama?"

"When I received the message, I requested that the sixth Dalai Lama be brought to my palace in Beijing. Something happened on the way and the sixth Dalai Lama never arrived. I then declared him to be an imposter and began the process of finding the real sixth Dalai Lama. Once this Dalai Lama was found, I built a place for him to stay at my palace when he was not ruling Tibet," said Chang. "It was my little butterfly who saved the faith, and brought Tibetan Buddhism to China. And she has come again to save the faith in this lifetime. "

My research has shown that Chang ultimately defeated all of the Mongolian tribes in Tibet and made it part of his empire in 1718. Contrary to popular belief, Tibet has remained a province of China for nearly three hundred years.

❀ Why Was I in the Tomb?

When I told Francesca of Chang's message about her ultimate fate in Tibet, she did not know what to do. It was all an amazing revelation for her. All she could do was cover her face with her hands and cry.

"This is just too much for me to take," she said between sobs. "I know why I wasn't in the tomb now. In Tibet they don't care about your dead body. They just cut you up and feed you to the vultures. They would never send my body back to China."

"Is there anything else you want to know?" I asked.

"There's one thing puzzling me," she said. "Ask Baba why you were buried in the tomb with him. I can understand why Brenda was there. She was an empress, but you were Chinese and not nobility. I really don't understand that at all."

"I don't know why either," I said. "It seems kind of strange to me, too."

"Maybe if you talk to Baba he'll tell you what happened," said Francesca.

"You may be right. Let me try," I replied.

I closed my eyes and began to meditate. I found Chang waiting for me.

"I knew you'd be back," he said.

"I have something else to ask you," I said.

"You want to know why you're in the tomb with my cocoon, don't you," he said, smiling.

"How did you know?" I asked.

"We know everything in heaven," said Chang smugly.

"Who was I, anyway?" I questioned impatiently.

Chang laughed at my impatience. "You were my teacher, Yong Loo. You were a respected Chinese scholar who taught me about many spiritual things. You taught me about Taoism, Buddhism, and Confucianism, and a lot more."

"But there were lots of scholars in China. Why would you choose me to be buried with you?" I asked.

Chang looked at me, shaking his head back and forth, and said, "Don't you remember anything, Keith?"

"No," I said. "I'm really confused by all of this. Please enlighten me."

"Well, Keith," Chang continued, "I respected you so much as a scholar, that I made you my Minister of Faith. You were in charge of all the religious rituals in China. You helped me with the Jesuits and their Christianity. You also assisted me in bringing the Tibetan Buddhist faith to China."

"But why am I in the tomb with you?" I asked.

"You saved my life, you helped bring peace to China, and you saved the Western world too," said Chang.

Surprised, I asked him how.

Chang just shook his head. "You still don't remember, do you Keith?" he said. "During my last visit to the city of Yangtze in the southern provinces, my son Yinreng, whom I had made the Crown Prince, and my son Yinxiang were influenced by some of my advisors to plot a coup against me. You heard about this plot, and at the risk of your own life, sent a message warning me about it. With your help I was able to defeat everyone who tried to get rid of me. If you hadn't warned me of this revolt, my incompetent son Yinreng would have taken over China."

"What would have happened if he had taken the throne?" I asked.

"My son was not prepared to lead China. He probably would not have seen the Mongol threat coming, and would have let them invade our country. If the Mongols had taken China, I am certain that they would have gone on to conquer Europe and the New World next," said Chang.

"Was this why I was buried with you?" I asked.

"Not exactly," replied Chang. "After my death in 1722, my son Prince Yingzhen took power against my wishes. Because of his illegal actions, Yingzhen was afraid that there might be a rebellion against him, led by his brothers and my former ministers."

"What did he do?" I asked.

"Yingzhen had many of my ministers arrested and executed. You were very close to me, so he feared your influence the most. He had you beheaded, first of all. I am sorry that you lost your life this way," said Chang.

"He was the person reincarnated as Renfield, the one who fired me from my job, wasn't he?" I said sadly.

"Yes, he was," Chang replied softly. "Your enemies always flock with you, along with your friends, in whatever lives you live."

"This still doesn't explain how I ended up in your tomb," I said insistently.

"Yingzhen knew how close you and I were, and he became concerned that my spirit might come back and do vengeful things to him for killing you. To appease my spirit, he had your body placed in my tomb with me and my empresses," said Chang.

"Had anything like this ever happened before?" I asked.

"You were the first non-royal to be buried with an emperor in China in over one thousand years. You were also the only Chinese person ever buried in the Qing tombs," said Chang.

"I think I understand now," I said. "That was really a great honor."

I later did historical research on the topics Chang had told me about. To my amazement, almost everything checked out exactly as he said. Chang's Chinese teacher was buried with him and his empresses in their tomb. There is little historical evidence about who this teacher was, or why he was buried with Chang.

I had no knowledge of Chinese history before I began writing this book, and now I know quite a bit about the subject. I not only did research about China, but I also learned that I was actually part of Chinese history.

I now know why Chang appears to me, and I feel honored when he says that I am the chosen one. I was chosen to bring the significance of Chinese history to the Western world. My mission in this lifetime is also to teach the world the lessons I have learned from Chang about peace and true love. I know that I will continue to learn more lessons as I walk my path and pursue my ongoing quest for Chang.

❀ Parallels in Time

As I did my research and wrote this book, I found that there were numerous things that Francesca and I had in common with the Kangxi emperor I call Chang. Here are some of the most remarkable coincidences we have discovered to date:

1. Chang (the Kangxi emperor) was born in 1654; Francesca was born in 1954.
2. Francesca's father's mother in this lifetime died when he was nine years old; Chang's mother died when he was nine years old.

3. Chang was raised by his grandmother; Francesca's father was raised by his grandmother.

4. Francesca's father's mother was named Panchita; Chang's grandmother was named Bochita.

5. Francesca was named for her father's mother Panchita; the Butterfly Princess was named for her father's grandmother Bochita.

6. Chang gave his daughter Bochita the nickname *Franchier* (this means swallowtail butterfly in Chinese); Francesca changed her name from Panchita to Francesca, which sounds very similar to *Franchier*, when she became a U.S. citizen in 1980.

7. The Butterfly Princess became a Buddhist nun in the seventeenth century; Francesca was accepted to become a Roman Catholic nun in this lifetime.

8. The Butterfly Princess lost her only child; Francesca lost her first grandchild.

9. Francesca was sent to the U.S. against her will by her parents when she was eighteen years old; the Butterfly Princess was sent to Mongolia against her will by her parents when she was sixteen years old.

10. Chang was proclaimed emperor of China on February 17; Francesca was born January 17; I was born October 17; our youngest son Kevin was born June 17; most of the things that Chang has told me about have happened in the seventeenth century; "The Butterfly Lovers" story took place 1700 years ago.

11. Within days of completing the first draft of this book, an exhibit titled "The Dragon Awakes: China from the Qing Dynasty to the Communist Revolution" opened at the Ventura County Museum of Natural History, just two blocks from our store. This exhibit consisted of dolls designed by artist George S. Stuart depicting the emperors of the Qing Dynasty (featuring Chang, the Kangxi emperor).

❀ Books

Allione, Tsultrim. *Women of Wisdom.* Ithaca, NY: Snow Lion
Publications, Inc., 2000.

Beckwith, Christopher I. *Tibetan Empire in Central Asia.* Princeton,
NJ: Princeton University Press, 1993.

Behr, Edward. *The Last Emperor.* London and Sydney: Macdonald
& Company, 1987.

Bold, B. *Mongolian Nomadic Societies.* London: Palgrave MacMillan
Publications, 1999.

Brown, J.D. *Frommer's Beijing, 2nd Edition.* London: Wiley
Publishing, Inc., 2002.

Browne, Sylvia. *Angels and Spirit Guides.* Carlsbad, CA: Hay
House, 2002.

Ebrey, Patricia Buckley. *Cambridge Illustrated History of China.*
Cambridge: Cambridge University Press, 1999.

———. *Chinese Civilization.* New York: The Free Press, 1993

Edward, John. *Understanding Your Angels and Meeting Your Guides.*
Carlsbad, CA: Hay House, 2000.

———. *Crossing Over.* Carlsbad, CA: Hay House, 2002.

Fairbank, John King. *China: A New History.* Cambridge, MA:
Harvard University Press, 1998.

Harrier, Heinrich. *Seven Years in Tibet.* East Rutherford, NJ:
Penguin Group, 1997.

Haw, Stephen G. *Travelers History of China.* North Hampton, MA:
Interlink Publishing Group, 2003.

Lama, The Dalai. *My Land My People*. New York: Warner Books, 1962.

———. *The Power of Compassion*. London: Harper Collins Publications, 2000.

Miller, Korina. *Lonely Planet Best of Beijing*. Oakland, CA: Lonely Planet Publications, 2004.

Morton, W. Scott. *China: Its History and Culture*. London: The McGraw Hill Companies, 2004.

Perdue, Peter C. *China Marches West: The Qing Conquest of Central Eurasia*. Cambridge, MA: Harvard University Press, 2005.

Roberts, J.A.G. *A Concise History of China*. Cambridge, MA: Harvard University Press, 1999.

Smith, Richard J. *China's Cultural Heritage 1644–1912*. New York: Westview Press, 1994.

Spence, Jonathan D. *Search for Modern China*. New York: W.W. Norton & Co., 1999.

Starr, John Bryan. *Understanding China*. New York: Hill and Wang Publications, 2000.

Twyman, James F. *Emissary of Light: My Adventures with the Secret Peace Makers*. New York: Warner Books, 1996.

Van Plas, Michel. *Lhasa in the Seventeenth Century*. Germantown, NY: Brill Academic Publications, 2003.

Van Praagh, James. *Talking to Heaven: A Medium's Message of Life After Death*. East Rutherford, NJ: Penguin Group, 1997.

Virtue, Doreen, Ph.D. *Past Life Regression with the Angels*. Carlsbad, CA: Hay House, 2004

Weiss, Dr. Brian. *Many Lives, Many Masters: The True Story of a Prominent Psychiatrist, His Patient, and the Past Life Therapy that Changed Both of Their Lives*. New York: Firestone, 1988.

Zhang, Qizhi. *The Chinese History—Yuan, Ming and Qing Dynasties*. Beijing: Chinese Higher Education Press, 2001.

✿ Internet Sites

China History to Qing Dynasty: East Asia Library
   www.usc.ed (search keywords above)

Easy Tour China
   www.easytourchina.com

Don Croner's Worldwide wanders: Mongolia/Life of Zanzibar
   www.doncroner.com

Electronic Passport to Chinese History
   www.mrdowling.com

Dreams of Tibet
   www.pbs.org/wgbh/pages

Genghis Khan, Web links to sites
   www.isidore-of-seville.com

History of Mongolia
   www.fpmt.org/mongolia/history.html

History of Tibet
   www.infoplease.com/ce6/world/Ao861546.html

Hypnosis and Past Life Regression
   www.spiritguides.info

Introduction to the History of Mongolia
   www.indiana.edu/~mongsoc/mong/history.htm

Kangxi Emperor of China
   www.infosearchpoint.com/display/Emperor_Kangxi

Liang Shanbo and Zhu Yingtai (Butterfly Lovers)
   http://en.wikipedia.org

Qing Dynasty
www.mnsu.edu/emuseum/prehistory/china/later_imperial_
china/qing.html

Qing Dynasty
http://pedia.nodeworks.com

Qing Dynasty: Ancient Chinese Dynasties
www.travelchinaguide.com

Reincarnation: Does The Bible Allow for this Possibility
www.christiananswers.net/q-eden/edn-r009.html

Reincarnation and The Bible
www.near-death.com/experiences/origen03.html

Reincarnation and The Bible
www.powerattunements.com

Spirit Guides
www.crystalinks.com

Spirit Guides
htpp://healingdeva.com

Spirit Guides
www.spiritguides.com

World Religions: Comparative Analysis
www.comparativereligion.com